Hexham Cemetery
A place of charm and historic interest

CONTENTS

Published for Hexham Town Council
by Hexham Local History Society

Foreword

Many fine cemeteries were constructed during the Victorian period and Hexham is very fortunate in having such a splendid example. The old burial ground around the Abbey became overfull and St Andrew's Cemetery was laid out in 1859 on the western outskirts of the town.

The Cemetery displays stylish symmetry with twin entrance buildings, twin chapels and an elegant row of Wellingtonia trees. Architectural detail abounds and a plaque commemorates the efforts of the founding fathers. A copy of St Acca's Cross, erected as a memorial to Isaac Baty, confronts the visitor. The style and variety of tombstones brings interest to the eye. The views to the north over the Tyne Valleys are stunning and the epitaphs on the many memorials tell fascinating tales of our forebears.

Hexham Town Council attaches much importance to its stewardship of the cemetery and is most grateful to David and Ruth Jennings, two members of Hexham Local History Society, for producing this fine informative booklet.

Michael Way
Mayor,
Hexham Town Council

The history of Hexham Cemetery

David Jennings

Introduction

Until the 19th century, all burials in Hexham took place in the two graveyards on the northern side of the Abbey Church. After St Mary the Virgin was built in 1830, Roman Catholics were buried in the small associated graveyard, the first burial being that of Thomas Leadbitter in 1833. However the numbers interred there were never more than around half a dozen in any one year. In contrast, deaths of members of the Church of England and other denominations by the mid-19th century were running at around 100 per year. Not surprisingly, graveyard space in the Abbey graveyard was becoming at a premium.

On 9 June 1854, there was a parochial visitation to Hexham by the Revd. George Bland, Archdeacon of Northumberland. He was met by the Incumbent, the Revd. Joseph Hudson, his Curate, the Revd. W. Franklin, and the Churchwardens, together with a group of town notables, such as William Wilson Gibson and William Robb. Among his several comments in a report to the Vestry about the state of the Church and the graveyard, Bland said

> I find the Church-yard very crowded and too confined for the
> use of the Parish, and I particularly recommend that in future
> non-parishioners be not buried in it

Robert Rawlinson in his 1853 report to the General Board of Health in London on the condition of the town and township had expressed a similar view, concluding that 'there is no township burial-ground adequate for the present and growing requirements of the place'

The eventual trigger for action was a letter to the Home Office from a local magistrate, John Ridley, 'calling attention to the crowded state of Hexham Church Yard' and requesting that an early opportunity will be taken of inspecting 'that Bl. Ground'. The request was transmitted by the Home Office to its Inspector, P. H. Holland, on 25 March 1857. He acted quickly, because, on 9 April, Joseph Hudson was given the details of what was to be the eventual Order-in-Council under the Burial Act 1853, dated 25 June 1857, by which burials were to be discontinued in Hexham forthwith beneath the *church of* Hexham, including the *Lady Chapel*; and from and after the first day of July 1858, in the churchyard, with the exception of now existing vaults and brick graves which can be opened without disturbing soil that has already been buried in, and in which each coffin shall be embedded in a layer of powdered charcoal, four inches thick and be separately entombed in brick or stone work properly cemented.

It was this decision that led to the establishment of the public cemetery in Hexham. But there were other factors favouring such cemeteries. One important consideration was the risk to health consequent on the burial of persons dying from infectious diseases. During the outbreak of cholera in Hexham in 1853, lime was liberally spread in the graveyard to minimise this risk. The only evidence that we have that this latter procedure was effective comes from a brief biography in the *Hexham Courant* of March 15th, 1930, of Johnie Gordon, the sexton at that time. Though having had an arduous time digging graves as a result of the cholera epidemic, Johnie 'was proof against infection'. In any case, many urban graveyards were severely overcrowded and as such were considered an affront to public decency. In particular, the location, if it was amidst the bustle of the centre of a town, as was the case in Hexham, militated against the last offices for the dead being conducted with the required degree of solemnity and impressiveness that came to be desired in the 19th century. In a more positive manner, a public cemetery if properly designed ought to enhance the burial ceremony and provide an uplifting environment in which to honour the dead. There were fine examples of such good design in Newcastle – Westgate Hill Cemetery (opened in 1829), Jesmond Old Cemetery (1836) and All Saints Cemetery, Jesmond (1856).

Establishment of a Burial Board

The Order-in-Council concentrated the minds of the Vestry such that on 29 July 1857 it resolved that 'a new Burial Ground be shall be provided for the township of Hexham' and on 12 August it established a Burial Board consisting of the following persons

Name	Occupation	Religious persuasion
George Bell	'Chymist'	Presbyterian Church
William Wilson Gibson	'Chymist'	Church of England

Matthew Ord	Clock and Watch Maker	Roman Catholic
William Pattinson	Tallow Chandler	Church of England
Thomas Pratt	Gentleman	Nonconformist
Edward Pruddah	Stationer	Congregationalist then Church of England
William Robb	Draper	United Methodist
James Spencer	Ironfounder	Possibly Congregationalist
William Wear	Timber Merchant	Church of England

The search for a site

Given the time scale of less than a year to have a new burial ground ready for burials, the Burial Board had to move quickly. Indeed, it started work on the same day as the Vestry meeting, when it decided that its first job was to establish a meeting place, who should be chairman and who should be appointed solicitor and clerk. It was resolved at the next meeting that William Robb should be Chairman and Isaac Baty was to be Solicitor and Clerk to the Board[1]. After that particular meeting the Burial Board met in the Board Room of the Local Board of Health in St Mary's Chare.

The formalities established, the Board devoted all its energies to searching for a site for the burial ground. The first site considered was at Fowl Bridge (the location of which is not clear), owned by Robert Bell, of High Shield, but that seemed to be too expensive. The next site was at Shaftoe Leazes owned by W. B. Beaumont but he was not willing to sell. The Board was to fail in its exploration of other possible sites at Broadway near Quatre Bras, Woodley Shield, Low Shield, Mill Riding (the location not clear) and at Halliwell Dene. However, the matter moved to a resolution on 26 October 1857 when a deputation from the Board met Mr John Grey, of Dilston, land agent for the Derwentwater estates, now belonging to the Commissioners of Greenwich Hospital. He intimated that, if the Board were to offer the Commissioners £640 for four acres of land at High Wood Farm, he would recommend them to sell at that price, taking upon themselves the compensation to their tenant. The next step was to examine the sub-soil of the site for its suitability as a burial ground. On 30 October, the Board met at the field for sale and inspected the pits that had been dug for them. The sub-soil was essentially a compacted gravel but there

---

[1] Derick Tiffin, the present Clerk to the Town Council, the body now responsible for the Cemetery, is with the firm of Robert Lewis & Co., Solicitors of Orchard Place, Hexham, the successors to the original firm of Baty and Fisher.

was some worry about the presence of large stones some four feet from the surface. In the end, further pits convinced the Board that the site had much to commend it. Its mind was made up when a trial at Mr Robert Bell's field at Fowl Bridge had to be stopped when the sub-soil had been excavated to a depth of two feet because of rising water.

On 23 November 1857, the vestry approved the purchase of the land, the Burial Board, being empowered to borrow £700 initially. The land itself was to cost £540 but in the end the Burial Board had to bear the expenses and charges relating to the sale, as well as compensation to the tenant of High Wood Farm, Mr William Todd, for his interest in the lease of the four acres that were sold.

The building of the Cemetery

While these negotiations were proceeding, on 23 December, the Chairman reported that Mr A. M. Dunn was soliciting appointment as Architect to the Board. He was appointed to that post on 23 February 1858. There was no evidence that any other architect was considered, which might be considered strange, particularly since Archibald Matthias Dunn (1832-1917) was only at the start of what was eventually to be a notable career. However, he had just completed the previous year the chapels for St Nicholas' Cemetery at Fenham in Newcastle (now 'horribly altered' according to Pevsner's *Northumberland* 2nd edn.). It was probably knowledge of these buildings that convinced the Board to appoint him. He attended the Board the next day after his appointment and, at that meeting, he was asked to prepare plans for two chapels, each of which were not to cost above £600, and two lodges, not to cost more than £300 each. The plans had to be ready by 16 March 1858.

The plans were ready on schedule. On 12 April, the plans together with the proposal to expend not more than £2,800 on the proposed buildings and the layout of the Cemetery were put before the Vestry. As the *Newcastle Chronicle* of 3 May 1858 has it

> Now one would have thought that when this cemetery was to be done it were better to do it well. Not so however. Several of the ratepayers would have the chapel like stables and the cemetery like a waste in the wilderness.

Those striving for economy (but really to keep the rates down) put forward an amendment that the sum to be expended should not exceed £1,800. This amendment was lost on a show of hands. At this result, Thomas Welford a perpetual fighter for reduced public expenditure, demanded that there be a poll of ratepayers on the proposal. According to the *Chronicle*, 'immediately the parties set to work to bring up their respective forces'. Polling took place over the next three days, the first two of which showed the opposition in the lead. 'But on the third day the Board bestirred themselves' and the proposal of the Burial Board was eventually carried by 367 votes to 207.

This victory in the poll triggered a number of key decisions. Tenders were invited for the building works, which included not only the buildings above but also an entrance gateway and boundary works. It was decided that the facing stone should come from the Prudhamstone quarry, rubble from any quarry except, interestingly, High Shield. The Vestry was later asked to, and indeed did authorise the borrowing of the necessary money (£2,800) for the building to take place as well as the laying out of the burial ground itself. That money and the £700 referred to earlier was eventually borrowed from local people on the security of the future poor rates of the Township. The Vestry also authorised the engaging of a Superintendent at a yearly salary of £45, together with a house and 'firing'.

There were a number of different trades associated with the building work, the major element being mason work and carving. Matthew Dodd of Gilesgate was awarded this contract at a price of £1320. Nineteen applications were received for the post of Superintendent. On 11 May 1858, Henry Robson was appointed to the post. The following week a Mr George Nixon was appointed clerk of works at a salary of £2 per week. Henry Robson, in a similar manner to Dunn, had also made an unsolicited application for this post, including several testimonials with the documents that he sent.

While all this was going on, it became obvious that the deadline of 1 July 1858 would not be met. The Home Secretary was persuaded to agree to the date 'for closing the Hexham Church Yard' should be extended to the 1 January 1859. At around the same time, the Bishop of Durham approved the proposed plans for the Cemetery. Thereafter work on the project proceeded apace. But still not fast enough, so that a further extension was requested. Up to 1 June 1859 was given, but no further extensions beyond that time were to be granted.

The grounds were laid out as we see them today. Edward Hutchinson ploughed and cleaned the ground. Shrubs were provided by John Robson, while Mr D.W. Rome laid out the grave spaces. The ground itself was divided into consecrated (for the internment of members of the Church of England) and unconsecrated areas (Fig. 1). One problem was the provision of a supply of water. Eventually, arrangements were made for water to be piped across Greenwich Hospital land from High Wood.

The opening of the Cemetery led to hardship for the sexton, Johnie Gordon, who was referred to earlier, since the source of his livelihood, payment for digging graves in the Abbey churchyard, was now cut off. He was now 68. Friends came to his rescue and a sufficient sum was collected to secure for him six shillings a week. Mr T. C. Maling of Westfield House and Mr J. O. Head were liberal contributors to the fund. Other assistance was at hand, for on 27 May the Burial Board agreed that John Oliver (a.k.a. Johnie Gordon) was to receive his fee of 1/6 for each grave made in the consecrated portion, paying it over to him 'without his being required to dig such graves'.

The functioning of the completed Cemetery

The cemetery was opened on 1 June 1859. The first body to be interred was, on the next day, of a child, Alan Lister, aged 14 months. Alan was the son of William Lister, a private in the Northumberland Artillery Militia, at this time stationed in Hexham.

To our eyes, now that the planting has matured and the old part of the cemetery almost completely occupied with graves, many with fine headstones and monuments, what must have looked very raw when completed, now looks very attractive and is a haven of tranquillity. James Stevens Curl in his book *The Victorian Celebration of Death* speaks about Hexham being 'a charming cemetery'. The entrance is suitably dignified with fine iron gates, those for vehicles set between two impressive pillars. Smaller gates, each set in walls, for pedestrians adjoin the two flanking lodges. The greater part of both walls of the lodges facing the person coming through the gates is blank. This expanse of blank wall, together with the arrangement of the gates, gives the entrance a considerable degree of dignity. On the wall of the west lodge is a tablet executed

---

Fig.1 (*across*) A copy of the ground plan of the original part of the Cemetery, showing the consecrated and unconsecrated parts. Both are divided into sections labelled A to D, and, though these sections are only lettered in the consecrated side of the plan, the equivalent sections in the unconsecrated side can be readily made out (reproduced by kind permission of Tynedale Council and Hexham Town Council – NRO/PBU/BS/1).

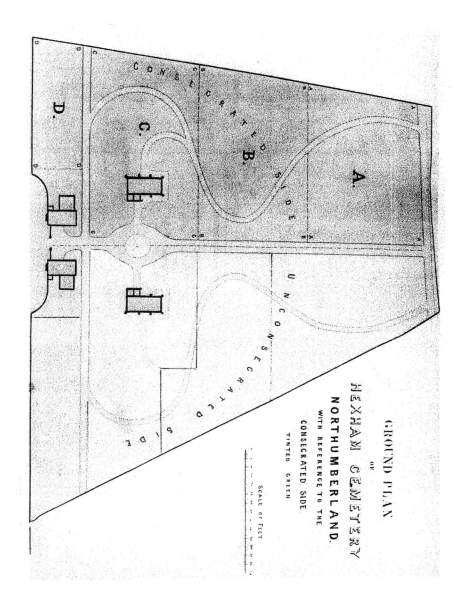

GROUND PLAN
OF
HEXHAM CEMETERY
NORTHUMBERLAND.
WITH REFERENCE TO THE
CONSECRATED SIDE
TINTED GREEN

SCALE OF FEET

CONSECRATED SIDE

UNCONSECRATED SIDE

A.

B.

C.

D.

8

THIS CEMETERY
WAS
BEGUN AND COMPLETED
IN 1858-9,
UNDER THE DIRECTION OF THE
FIRST BURIAL BOARD
OF THE
TOWNSHIP OF HEXHAM,
WILLIAM ROBB, *Chairman*
WILLIAM WEAR
WILLIAM W. GIBSON
JAMES SPENCER
EDWARD PRUDDAH
THOMAS PRATT
WILLIAM PATTINSON
MATHEW ORD
GEORGE BELL
ISAAC BATY, *Clerk*
ARCHIBALD M. DUNN
Architect.

and delivered to Hexham at the cost of the Architect, A. M. Dunn, giving details of the Burial Board (Fig. 2). The two chapels (one no longer used for services) are made more impressive with their spires and stand well on the slight eminence above a sloping burial ground (Fig. 3, *page 12*). Pevsner in his *Northumberland* asks us to note 'lots of ornament and the chapels have quiet and pious faces on the widow hood mould stops, in contrast to the grotesques on the adjacent buttresses'. The two chapels are now visually linked through a central feature, a reconstruction of Acca's Cross, a monument to the solicitor Isaac Baty (1849-1894), made by Charles C. Hodges and carved by Robert Beall.

Once the fabric and layout of the Cemetery was complete, the Burial Board could confine its attention to overseeing the functioning of the Cemetery, selling plots and deciding on the suitability of any proposed grave monuments. The rules for the Cemetery had been established before it was opened. It is interesting to compare what was drafted in 1859 with what is in the present information leaflet. Today's instructions are written in a relaxed style for the simple reason that well-established professionals are involved in burials, such as the monumental sculptor in the provision of gravestones and monuments and the undertaker who will oversee the funeral arrangements. It is these professionals who deal with the cemetery authorities. In contrast, the first rules were very prescriptive, almost certainly to ensure that there could be no misunderstanding by anybody of what was required. There have been a few significant changes over the one hundred and forty odd years. There has been a little softening of the rules about dogs in the cemetery. In the first rules 'No person will be allowed to take a dog into the grounds.' Today 'dogs are not permitted in the cemetery without prior permission from the Cemetery Superintendent. Dogs must be on a lead at all times.' In 1859 the cemetery was open at 6.00 a.m. to sunset on weekdays in the summer and 8.00 a.m. to sunset in the winter. On Sundays opening was delayed to 1.00 p.m. throughout the year. At the present time, the cemetery opens at the later hour of 9.00 a.m. throughout the year, closure being at 7.00 p.m., or dusk, if sooner, in the summer and 5.00 p.m. or dusk, if sooner, in the winter. Perhaps the most significant change since 1859 relates to the days on which internments took place. When the Cemetery was opened internments could take place on every day of the week, in particular on Sundays. We know now from a report in the *Hexham Courant* of 28 September 1901, that the Board thought that it was in the interests of the working class to allow internments on that particular day, because there were only a few from this class who could

Fig. 2 (*across*) Tablet designed by the architect on the entrance wall of the west lodge.

spare the time to attend funerals except on Sundays. This rule was maintained in spite of a petition signed by ministers of the town against it. Today, internments take place only on Mondays to Fridays.

With the opening of the Cemetery, the energies of the Burial Board were essentially devoted to approving the design of the monuments. A few examples of those, erected during the period from 1859 until the end of the 19th century, can be seen in some of the illustrations that accompany this text.

However, the Board had to deal with two important matters relating to the proper maintenance of the Cemetery. The first concerned the spires on the two chapels that were found to be too heavy and were endangering the roof of each building. They were said to be replaced in 1861 with lighter ones of similar design. But, in view of the fact that the spire on the eastern chapel (Fig. 4, *page 13*) is far more ornate than that of the west (which is of smaller volume and has a more pared down design), one wonders whether both spires were replaced. The visual evidence suggests only that of the west chapel had to be replaced, the spire of the east chapel appearing to be as first designed. Second, it seems that there was a continuing problem of surface water running through the cemetery. This problem was resolved in 1881 by expenditure of £100 on a new drain.

Control of the Cemetery vested in the Urban District Council

By 1901, after a series of Burial Acts, it became possible for the Hexham Urban District Council to take over the running of the Cemetery. Indeed in June of the same year, Councillor Ralph Conkleton raised the matter at a Council meeting. However he could not get anyone to second his proposal. Whatever the merits of Conkleton's case, there was certainly the feeling in the Council at that time that it was inappropriate to take action until a loan that the Burial Board had contracted had been paid off. But one person's action put the Burial Board in a new light. On 2 July 1901, E. W. Robson of 32 Fore Street, Hexham wrote to the Local Government Board in London complaining that there had not been an election for over ten years and second that at the present time no more than six (when there should have been nine) members constituted the Board. Thus these men had been spending money without the sanction of the public. The Burial Board defended its position by letter to the Local Government Board.

Fig.3 (*across*) The west chapel, which is still in use as such. The plain nature of the spire should be compared with that of the highly decorated spire of the east chapel shown in Fig. 4 (*page 13*).

11

Nevertheless a meeting was called and a properly constituted Board was elected. At the same meeting the then Chairman of the Burial Board, County Councillor William Alexander, put up a spirited defence of its actions. However, from the tenor of the remarks that he made, one has the feeling that a number of people in Hexham were not too happy with some of the actions of the Burial Board.

Nevertheless it was some while before the matter again came into the public arena. It was June 1908; Councillor Conkleton again raised the matter in the Urban District Council. Essentially his argument revolved round the undemocratic nature of the Burial Board. Though details of the actual procedure used for the election of the Board have not come to light, Conkleton indicated that a system of plural voting was still being used. This was in contrast to procedure, established in 1894, used for the election for the Urban District Council in which each elector had one vote. Further, the money for the Cemetery was supposed to be collected through the Poor Rate (though the collection did not always take place). Conkleton felt that, if the ratepayers paid for the Cemetery through the rates, the elected members ought to have management of it. But, unfortunately for Conkleton, what he proposed was inopportune at that particular time. As pointed out by the Chairman of the Council, James T. Robb, delicate negotiations were going on with respect to the acquisition of additional land for the Cemetery. Though the decision could be taken as a set-back for Conkleton, the leader writer of the *Hexham Courant* was confident that transfer of the powers of the Burial Board to the Urban District Council would not be long in coming. Later in 1908, it seemed that the need for additional land for the Cemetery was much less pressing than had been thought originally. In view of this, not too surprisingly, the Urban District Council on 4 January 1909 unanimously agreed to the transfer of duties of the Burial Board to the Council.

There was some delay before the Council took *de facto* control, which was to be through a standing committee. One major change was an active role of the Council's Surveyor, then G. L. Murray, in the running of the Cemetery and taking the title of Superintendent.

Extension of the Cemetery

It would only be a matter of time before it became imperative to obtain additional land for the Cemetery. Indeed, at the 30 March 1915 meeting of the

Fig. 4 (*across*) The spire of the east chapel. *See Fig. 3 and accompanying text for further details.*

Council, it was reported that the Cemetery Committee had accepted an offer from J. C. Straker for three acres of land, across the Carlisle Road, on the south side of the Cemetery, at a cost of £1,200. Previously, Straker had offered land to the west of the Cemetery. It is almost certain that the War prevented this plan from being executed. However, when the war ended, on 1 September 1919, the above decision was reversed and it was decided that negotiations be entered into with owners of land on both the west and east sides of the Cemetery. There were good reasons for this change of mind, namely the cost of putting a wall round the property on the other side of the road and the poor drainage of the site.

This new decision caused alarm amongst the golfing fraternity. Hexham's first golf club opened in 1888 on Tyne Green but the course proved unattractive to the enthusiasts. In 1907, they moved to a course, designed by Harry Vardon and J. S. Caird, to the west of the Spital, which was then the private residence of J. J. Kirsopp. Extension of the Cemetery could mean a reduction in the size of the course, seemingly in the loss of the 8th and 11th greens. A deputation met the Council and there was much correspondence on the matter in the local press. At the beginning of 1920, it was learnt that J. C. Straker was willing to sell two acres of land, leased to the Golf Club, for £400 'provided it [the purchase] is desired by the majority of ratepayers'. With what the *Hexham Courant* called 'cool audacity', the Cemetery committee recommended that 'Surveyor be instructed to prepare necessary plans and estimates for submission to the Ministry of Health.' However, in view of the proviso of J. C. Straker, wiser councils prevailed and the matter was delayed a month for a poll taken of ratepayers. The Clerk proceeded to draft a voting card for the next meeting of the Council. At that particular meeting, it was decided that the Surveyor should prepare plans for the extension of the Cemetery to the west comprising of two acres and to the south comprising of three acres. In the meantime, the issue of voting papers was to stand over until the information was available from the Surveyor. When it was available at the April meeting, it was clear that development on the south side was far too expensive compared to the west side - £1,000 per acre for the former; £300 for the latter. Not even the Golf Club could argue against those figures. Extension of the Cemetery took place to the west. The Golf Club, at a cost of £200, rearranged the two holes affected by the loss of land. According to Les Barrett author of the centenary history of the Club, *From Tyne Green to Spital: 1892-1992* 'the row which threatened to split the town ended in barely a whimper.'

Not surprisingly, with the country still severely affected by the financial cost of the 1914-18 War, there was a difference of opinion between the Urban District

15

Council and the Ministry of Health over the money that could be borrowed to incorporate the new land into the existing cemetery. The initial cost of the proposed work was put at £1625. In the end, the Council had to settle for £1,125. Initially, it was proposed to extend the wall along the southern edge of the new ground. The presence of a hedge there today is testimony to the economies that had to be made because of the lack of funds. Not quite half of the new land was allotted for the Church of England, a portion to the Roman Catholics and the remainder to the Nonconformists. On Monday, 31 August 1925, the Church of England portion was consecrated, on behalf of the Bishop of Newcastle, by the Very Rev. C. J. Wood, of St George's, Jesmond and formerly Bishop of Melanesia. From that date until the 1939-45 War, the running of the Cemetery was a relatively smooth operation. The only matter of concern came to the surface in 1938 when it was proposed to double the fees for burials on Sundays. After a considerable discussion, revolving round the extent to which the Council was subsidising the Cemetery, the matter of raising the fees for Sunday burials was eventually dropped.

The 1939-45 War and afterwards

During the 1914-18 War, ten members of the armed forces came to be buried in the Cemetery, their graves in scattered positions. However, at the start of the 1939-45 War, the Ministry of Health requested that a separate portion of the Cemetery be set aside for similar burials. As one walks from the north along the western edge of the original section of the Cemetery, it is not difficult to spot the area where the bulk of the graves of those who died on active service on behalf of King and Country are located (Fig. 5, *page 18*). In that area, there are several rows of white stones to the standard design of the Imperial War Graves Commission, each carrying the crest of the regiment or service, service number, rank, name, age of the person buried and their date of death. There are 21 such graves, one of which commemorates Bronislaw Plarsake, a member of the Polish Armed Forces.

What is less well known is that, for a period, the Cemetery has held the graves of those of other nationalities who fought both with us and against us. There were three French servicemen buried in the Cemetery. In 1948, a team from a London firm of funeral directors exhumed their remains. It is not known whether the bodies were returned to France or re-buried in one of the central cemeteries in this country. In 1958, the remains of two Italian prisoners of war were exhumed and transferred to Brookwood Military Cemetery in Surrey. Finally, in 1962, the remains of twelve German prisoners of war were exhumed and transferred back

16

to their native land.

In 1946, it became clear that, yet again, that accommodation for burials in the Cemetery was becoming inadequate. As well as considering how best to expand, the Council gave its first thoughts to the possibility of building a crematorium. It came closest to realisation in 1951 when the Surveyor suggested how one might proceed. That a chapel might be converted to a crematorium was ruled out, because it was not the requisite distance from the highway. But the cost was a forbidding barrier to surmount if a crematorium was to be built - £40,000 in 1951. Nevertheless, as late as 1968, the Surveyor to the Council, R. Stroughair, included a crematorium in the plans that he prepared for the most recent extension of the Cemetery. As we know the crematorium never materialised. Even in the 1980s, the suggestion of a crematorium was investigated yet again. It was finally deleted from future plans because the cost against the number of cremations that might take place showed it to be uneconomic.

At first, the moves to secure additional accommodation, which began in earnest in 1949, followed similar lines to those taken when the Cemetery was first extended in 1920-21. The Hexham Golf Club were very much against any extension to the west, saying that to lose the land would be 'affect the activities of the Club to a very large extent. It is felt that the growth of membership will be checked, [and] the revenue will be gravely affected...' As before, attention then focussed on the land the south on the other side of the main road. However, not only did the owner not wish to sell, because of its agricultural value, but the County Planning Officer was of the opinion that it would be preferable to obtain land on the same side of the road. Thoughts of acquiring the land on either side of the road by compulsory purchase were dashed by the Ministry of Health informing the Council that such purchase could only be justified on the grounds of emergency. The Ministry were of the opinion that there was enough space for burials to continue for another ten years. Only when the period had been reduced to two years should the application be renewed. In 1950, the County Council refused permission to use land on the opposite side of the road because it would necessitate crossing a trunk road.

However, matters took a considerable turn for the better in 1950, when Hexham Golf Club wrote to the Council asking it to indicate its policy with regard to the extension of the Cemetery before the Club undertook works of improvement and

Fig. 5 (*across*) The major portion of the graves of the members of the armed forces who were killed in the Second World War.

reconstruction of the course. The planning of these developments was the prelude to the purchase by the Golf Club of the Spital estate in 1951 and the expansion to its present size. By the end of 1951, with the sanction of the Ministry of Health, 1.3 acres to the west had been purchased and work on making the land ready for burials was almost complete. Part of the land was to be reserved as a lawn cemetery, in that no kerbs or dressings be allowed for economy of maintenance. This layout is standard for the newer parts of the Cemetery.

In 1967, the need for a still further extension became apparent yet again. This time the amount of land under consideration was considerable; at 17.2 acres, it was well over twice area of the then present cemetery. Not surprisingly, since there was a chance that this acreage of land might contain areas of unsuitable substrata, Cementation Co. was employed to sink boreholes to confirm that all the land was suitable for burial purposes. Negotiations then commenced with the Golf Club and approval was sought from the appropriate authorities. All seemed to go smoothly, nevertheless it was 1971 before work commenced on the extension, H. N. Marsh (Contracts) Ltd. of Birtley initiating the work at a tender price of £23,657. The work appears to have been completed in 1973.

Hexham Town Council becomes responsible for the Cemetery

Following the Local Government Act of 1972, reorganisation in 1974 led to the formation of Tynedale District Council and Hexham Town Council and the disappearance of the Urban District Council. Initially, there was an uneasy relationship between the two new authorities over the control of the Cemetery. Though there seemed to be doubts at first, in law the Town Council, initially known as Hexham Parish Council, was the statutory burial authority. Tynedale Council, though, had not really wanted to relinquish control of any assets and had taken over the deployment of labour for the general maintenance and running of the Cemetery. There was thus some confusion in the division of responsibility. The situation was resolved in 1975 by the establishment of a formal agency agreement between the Town Council and the District Council in which the former took over all the administration with respect to burials and the latter remained responsible for the deployment of labour and maintenance. A consultative joint cemeteries sub-committee was established that included members of Tynedale District Council and both the Town Councils of Hexham and Prudhoe (which also had its own cemetery). However, as early as the next year, a sub-committee of the Town Council was proposing that it should assume full control of the Cemetery, though it would mean some capital cost to the

Council such as the purchase of a mechanical digger and a much larger (36 inch) grass cutter. In the event, full control did not take place until 1984, when the present Clerk of the Town Council finally persuaded the Council that the cost of employing Tynedale Council to manage the Cemetery would be saved if it ran it itself.

Since then there have been two imaginative developments in the Cemetery. The first was when, in 1995, the Council created a Woodland Burial section. It was one of the first such burial grounds in this country and is still one of the very few in Northumberland. Beside this section, the Pet Cemetery was established in 1996 for the burial of pets. The second came to fruition in 2001 when the Millennium was commemorated with the construction of a sheltered seat with a superb view up the North Tyne Valley.

Sources of information

For the period up to the Cemetery being taken over by the Urban District Council, I have relied on the minute book of the Burial Board now in the Northumberland Record Office (NRO/PHU/B1/6 & 7), though to obtain details of how the Abbey graveyard was closed I had to go to the Public Record Office (PRO/HO/85/9). From about 1900 until 1974, the major source of information was the *Hexham Courant* and the minute books of the Urban District Council (NRO/LHU/A1). The Public Record Office provided details of the negotiations with the Ministry of Health concerning the first extension of the Cemetery (PRO/HLG/45/699). For the years subsequent to 1974, I referred to the minute books of Hexham Town Council (NRO/PC/65) and Tynedale District Council (DTD/A1) and was particularly helped by those documents relating to the assumption of full control by the Town Council (NRO/PC65/15). The following books were consulted; those by Curl and Morgan, particularly the former, provide background information the 19th-century cemetery movement:

Barrett, L (n.d.) *From Tyne Green to Spital: 1892-1992.* Published privately
Curl, J. S. (2000) *The Victorian Celebration of Death.* Sutton Publishing: Thrupp, Stroud.
Grundy, J., McCombie, G., Ryder, P., Welfare, H. and Pevsner, N. (1992) *Northumberland.* Penguin Books: London.
Morgan, A. (2000) *A Fine and Private Place: Jesmond Old Cemetery.* Tyne Bridge Publishing: Newcastle upon Tyne.

I am most grateful to Derick Tiffin, John Thirlwell and Michael Way for other much helpful information.

Superintendents of the Cemetery

Henry Robson 1858-1899
J. W. Westcott 1899-1910
G. L. Murray* 1910-1913
J. W. Pooley* 1913-1922
W. G. Landale* 1922-1946
W. A. Hancocks* 1946-1966

R. Stroughair* 1966-1976
A. Scott 1976-1980
R. Turner 1980-1997
J. Thirlwell 1997-present

* Surveyor to the Hexham Urban District Council

Hexham Parish Council

Chairman
J. P. Pickering 1974-5

Clerk of the Council
Athol Bates 1974

Hexham Town Council

Mayors
J. P. Pickering 1975-6
John McG. Pescott 1976-7
Francis J. Young 1977-8
John McG. Pescott 1978-9
Evan D. Huntingdon 1979-80
Donald M. Jowett 1980-2
Richard J. Boaden 1982-4
John Mc G. Pescott 1984-6
H. John C. Herron 1986-8
Ian T. Hepple 1988-90

John P. Lynch 1990-3
Francis J. Young 1993-4
William Moulding 1994-5
Mrs Catherine A. Clark 1995-6
Norman J. Reed 1996-7
Brian Waters 1997-8
Philip Clark 1998-9
Mrs Audrey Hutchinson 1999-2000
George C. Ferguson 2000-1
Michael Way 2001-present

Clerks to the Council
John S. Hart-Jackson 1974-7

Derick Tiffin 1977-present

Burials in the original part of Hexham Cemetery

Ruth Jennings

Burials started in newly constructed Cemetery in June 1859 and continued there regularly up to the opening of the first extension, to the west, in 1925. Even then, spaces in the oldest part of the Cemetery were still being used, especially in those graves purchased by families, right through the 20th century. Though the practice of cremation came in with the Act of 1902, the Burial Board was anxious to use (and profit from) every square foot of available space and we estimate the 2 or 3 acres of old Cemetery must have contained between 10,000 and 15,000 burials.

But though the constant opening and reusing of burial spaces may strike us today as quite unacceptable, the organisation and management of the new Cemetery was according to the latest rules and regulations. These were framed as the result of the sweeping reforms brought in by legislation in the mid-nineteenth century. Official reports of the 1830s and 1840s had been showing how burial in the old, overcrowded churchyards was both insanitary and undignified. The norm was an uncharted space where paupers or those dying in epidemics were thrown into open pits. The gentry might be able to reserve and mark for themselves a family plot but even then the digging of graves invariably brought to the surface bones 'or worse'. In built-up areas, with dwellings close to old burial grounds, the ground surface gradually rose and inspectors were regularly told of seepage from retaining walls, bad smells and health problems. The government responded with a series of Burial Acts supported by regulations from the Public Board of Health. Just how bad was the Abbey Churchyard in Hexham, we shall never know – we have not been able to find a copy of the inspector's report of 1858 – but, as David Jennings has explained, it was condemned that year and closed in 1859.

So it was that when the Hexham Cemetery was being planned in 1858 the members of the Burial Board were supplied with, and recommended to read, Scott's and Baker's *Burial Acts*. These books we have not been able to trace but with gleanings from various Acts of Parliament and later accounts of burial practice it is clear that the rules provided for, basically, two sorts of burial in graves which had to be carefully laid out and mapped; that is, a) in a purchased or private grave or b) in a public or communal grave.

a) From the start of graveyard regulation in the early 19th century, there were elaborate rules for the sale of *private grave space*, as for any legal transaction that involved property. In its Rules of 25 October 1858 the Hexham Burial Board specified, for 'Ground purchased in Perpetuity', a charge of 40/- for a space 9 ft. by 4 ft. To construct a vault the buyer had to pay 80/- and to erect a monument, 10/-. These charges did not include the cost of construction, interment charges (see below) or, of course, funeral expenses.

b) For interment in a *communal grave*, those who wished to choose among the available spaces were charged on a scale of 5/- to 10/-, according to the age of the deceased (under 7, over 7, over 16). If the choice of location was left to 'the Board', the charges were 3/- to 5/- (with 2/- for stillborn infants). This category of burial was obviously designed for poorest people in the town who needed this least expensive option. If they wished to be placed near their kin, it was possible to reserve spaces for up to 14 years for a further charge and this was often done, say, for a husband and wife. Pauper burials, at the expense of the parish, were charged at the minimum rate.

The Board did not publish in its Rules, nor apparently discuss in its meetings at this early stage, the government regulations that concerned the dimensions of graves, the spacing of interments, and the restrictions on successive occupancy. These rules emanated from the Board of Health that was concerned about drainage and the time taken for coffins and bodies to decompose. Thus, when Hexham Cemetery was laid out, adult grave spaces had to be 4ft. by 9ft. and children's (under 12) 3ft. by 6ft. with further stipulations about depths and spaces between and above coffins. The Hexham Burial Board settled for the basic unit space of 4ft. by 9ft. while, in practice, keeping adult and children's graves largely separate, putting 4 adults together and usually 8 but up to 10 or 11 children in one grave.

The rules were also quite specific about the time which should elapse between one burial in a grave space and the next, forbidding a second burial in an adult grave within 14 years and in a child's grave within 8. These times were later extended. A cursory look at the Grave Registers shows that adults, in Hexham Cemetery, were rarely if ever buried successively within the forbidden periods but that children were regularly 'doubled up' within days or weeks within one grave. The justification for this seems to have been that using graves of adult size, just twice the area for a child, it was possible to put two small children side by side, the second not disturbing the first. It is likely this practice was widespread and not questioned by the authorities. These rules, incidentally, did

23

not apply to 'members of the same family' so that in a purchased grave the burials could follow each other as the deaths in the family occurred.

We can now turn to the question of the social nuances of the different kinds of burial. The better-off, using private graves and usually erecting headstones, tend to receive the most attention if only because we know so much more about them. Their monuments often included mention of earlier ancestors (buried in the Abbey churchyard for instance) or relatives who had died elsewhere. Those of higher social status often merited an obituary in the *Hexham Courant* (from 1864) often with a detailed and much longer account of the funeral. How the rest of the populace arranged their burials is less clear; in particular, were those paid for by 'the parish' – the so-called pauper burials – kept separate from all the others in the communal graves? We know there was a considerable stigma attached to a parish burial but was this reflected in the Cemetery organisation in any way? The short answer seems to be that in certain areas of the Cemetery there were planned sequences of communal graves and that many paupers can be identified within these areas, but a careful look at the identities of those buried with them suggests that these graves were not strictly set aside for paupers, even in the early years.

That said, it is difficult to come to any firm conclusions about the management of pauper burials; the Hexham records, it seems, are as scanty as elsewhere. The Webbs' magisterial account of the English Poor Law (published in 1929) describes how the burial of the poor was an ancient duty of the parish and in late 19th-century Hexham we can see how most of the identifiable paupers were laid to rest in the Consecrated portion of the Cemetery by clergy of the Established Church. But the Webbs commented on the lack of documentation on local practice and certainly in Hexham no paupers are identified as such in any of the Cemetery registers. Some can be spotted as dying "in the workhouse" and there must have been others among those whose burials were paid for at the lowest rate. It is unfortunate that the Grave Registers state the fee paid but not who paid it.

However, we know that the Board of Guardians was responsible not only for the inmates of the workhouse but also for a variable number of men, women and children on outdoor relief in the wider parish and for the burial of anyone dying without friends or kin or any provision for burial expenses – or indeed for any casual or vagrant who might die within the parish boundaries. So one might have expected the Guardians' accounts to show a regular item for 'burials' but ledgers seen in the Northumberland Record Office only mention charges for the occasional 'indoor funeral', presumably for favoured employees. Consequently, we do not even have a rough idea of the total parish burials in successive years.

This leaves us dependent on the biographical details given in the Burial Register to try and pick out, from these communal graves, any persons who might be or were clearly not paupers. Among those likely to be paupers were the rather numerous babies and children of 'single women' (though this designation was dropped entirely in 1892) and other 'possibles' were the very old. At the same time it seems unlikely that young men with a stated occupation, or their dependents, were paupers and one early example would seem to clinch the matter. In Section D on the Consecrated side of the Cemetery a young man called James Hay was buried in 1876. At the time of his death, he was the Local Board of Health's Inspector of Nuisances and Surveyor, with a wife and family, earning £100 a year, and his death was marked with a short obituary in the *Hexham Courant*. He was clearly no pauper but he was placed, presumably with his widow's approval, in a communal grave where the previous interment was that of an 89 year-old man from the workhouse. It is possible, too, to pick out among the numerous children's burials apparent social mixtures in almost any grave. And there are (adult) communal graves here and there where the top two spaces have actually been purchased, lying over two apparently unrelated people.

All this suggests there was an agreed policy to offer categories of burial at a range of prices but not to mark out the paupers from the rest. How many of those arranging interment in communal graves actually enquired about previous occupants we shall never know, but as time went on it must have been accepted that the Cemetery staff could not tell you more than the names and details in the Registers – and perhaps very few were concerned even to ask. It certainly would have made economic sense for the Board to allow the distinctions to be blurred, for if they had marked out distinct pauper enclaves, because of the time rules, they might have found themselves opening a number of graves which were never filled. Perhaps, as Christian gentlemen, they just felt it right and proper to treat all as equal in their last resting places.

With all these considerations in mind we can now look at some of the features of the lay-out of graves in the original part of Hexham Cemetery (Fig. 1, *see page 8*). To start with, it is obvious that, while there are several hundred gravestones marking private graves, these are not evenly distributed around the available space. The bare, grassed areas show where the Board, from time to time, opened sequences of communal graves. These are most obvious in sections A and D in

25

the Consecrated half of the Cemetery but rows of communal graves were also opened in B (Consecrated) and in A, B and D on the other side. The two C sections, near the top of the graveyard alongside the chapels seem to have had some isolated communal graves but most of the graves here were private.

One more important feature of the new regime should be mentioned. It is marked by the end of nonconformist grievances about their right to conduct funerals. In a churchyard the incumbent held sway and though he would usually be willing to arrange a Christian burial, the Anglican form of words was often not acceptable to members of the well-established nonconformist sects. Hexham, by 1859, had Methodist, Presbyterian and Congregationalist churches, among others, and in the new Cemetery, under the new rules, half the available space was set aside for them as Unconsecrated. Here, any form of ceremony could be used, as long as it was decent and orderly, and the Burial Registers show how not only established ministers of these denominations officiated at burials but also large numbers of lay people. In the Consecrated area, to the west, those officiating were always the Abbey staff or Anglican clergy from elsewhere.

This sensitive regard for the feelings and rights of individuals and families at the time of death and burial was just one of the signs of the major social advance which the new cemeteries and the new burial practices brought in during the 19th century. The Hexham Cemetery stands as a monument to the efforts of the worthy gentlemen who planned, laid out, administered and maintained the Cemetery, following these more civilised working practices to the great benefit of the local community.

I am most grateful to Phil Thirkell who computerised the contents of first Cemetery Register (1859-1903), allowing a thorough analysis of selected grave plots. Copies of this register can be seen in Hexham Library and the Northumberland Record Office.

Biographies of some of those who are buried in the original part of the Cemetery

David Jennings

These biographies relate only to the original section of the Cemetery. It is only for this part that the monumental inscriptions have been recorded and computerised, allowing ease of access to the information about who has been buried and where. Further, this section has a degree of coherence increasingly lacking as time has gone by. When the Cemetery was opened in 1859, those who were buried in this section had for the most part lived their whole lives in Hexham and in doing so often contributed to the life of the town. Thus, those who are buried in this particular section represent a large part of a relatively tight-knit community. As time has gone on, the people have increasingly moved in and out of the area, while public bodies outwith the town, rather than private citizens within it, have had had a greater influence on the life of the Hexham. Meanwhile, the town has grown and become much more residential, with many working in Newcastle and other areas outside. All this means that, as the Cemetery has developed, the resting places of those who had a role in the life of the town, equivalent to those buried in the original part are increasingly scattered within it. Further such persons may have retired away from Hexham or may have been cremated. Thus, for later parts of the Cemetery, it proved very difficult to generate a set of biographies that was in any way representative. It has not helped that, as time has gone by, publication of obituaries of local personages has become much less frequent. Also, it must be noted that it has been very difficult to obtain information for persons whose deaths occurred prior to 1864, the year when the *Hexham Courant* was established.

So for the above reasons it was decided to confine the biographies to those buried in the original section of the Cemetery. I believe that those presented not only record the lives of notable personages but also give a picture of Hexham in the nineteenth century and the early part of the last. However, one should note that few Catholics are present amongst those buried in the original section, since burials were still taking place in St Mary's Catholic Churchyard[1]. Further, we know that some of the more notable persons who are buried are without a headstone.

---

[1] Burials continued in the Catholic Churchyard until 1933 but an increasing number were taking place in the Cemetery before that date.

Note: It has not been possible to obtain the dates of birth for all the entries. A '?' for a particular entry indicates that a date of birth is not available. In these circumstances, the age at death is given so that a possible date of birth can be calculated. The number in the second set of brackets indicates on the map that area in the Cemetery where the person concerned is buried (Fig. 6, page 30). The number bears no relation to any number given in the official records or on the map in the Cemetery Office.

John Ainsley (?-1933; 75) (20) – Painter and decorator. Born in Hexham, he served his apprenticeship with John Guthrie (*qv*), painter and paperhanger in Fore Street. He spent some time in South Shields before returning to work again for John Guthrie. When he died in 1890, Ainsley with an old colleague, James Graham, took over the business. Ainsley retired from the partnership in 1914 but continued to work for the firm. He was a man of many parts. He was a fine shot and a regular member of teams from the 1st Volunteer Battalion Northumberland Fusiliers and the Territorials. He made his name as a wrestler and was one of the original members of the Hexham Rowing Club. He was an exhibitor of cats, winning prizes at many shows. He was elected a member of the Hexham Urban District Council in 1901 and, apart from a short break, was a member till his death. As a Councillor he had an independent outlook and, in debate, had the ability to make his view known succinctly.

Joseph Alexander (?-1921; 81) (4) – Tanner and woolstapler. Born in Hexham, son of William Alexander, watchmaker and jeweller of Fore Street and a member the 'Lamp and Watch Committee' that was in existence prior to the formation of the Local Board of Health. Joseph Alexander owned the Hextol tannery, which used to be in what is now the square behind Tanners Row. He was active in the government of Hexham, being elected to the District Council when it was first established in 1894 and was elected its first chairman. He left the Council in 1901. He was a Guardian and early in his life a member of the 1st Company of the Hexham Rifle Corps. His obituary in the *Courant* speaks of him as 'leaving Hexham'. Certainly, he died in Newcastle. His exodus to that city may have been a consequence of him becoming bankrupt in 1908.

William Alexander (1842-1914) (25) – Initially provision merchant, later fruitgrower. He was the brother of Joseph Alexander (*qv*). William Alexander started in business in partnership with John Lisle that carried on the old-established firm of, Messrs John Grey & Son, provisions merchants. But he had other business interests. He took over his father's business when he died until it

28

was transferred to William Hope. He was for a long time interested in fruit growing, sending consignments of small fruits to Newcastle and other markets. After severing his interest in the firm of John Grey & Son, he acquired further acres of land, such that he had substantial holdings in the Tyne valley. As a result he expanded into apple growing, for which he had conspicuous success. Not surprisingly he was a highly respected member of Royal English Arboricultural Society. His contribution to the government of Hexham and Northumberland has hardly been equalled. It was as William Alexander Jr. that he was elected to the Local Government Board in 1876, becoming Chairman in 1883. He left the Board the following year. He returned to the affairs of the town in 1901, when he headed the poll for election to the Urban District Council, remaining until 1907, when he was surprisingly defeated in the election. He was Chairman for the period 1903-7. When, in 1910 the ward system for council elections came into being, he was elected once more to the Council, in this instance to represent the Priestpopple Ward. He became Chairman of the Council in 1913 and was in that post when he died. Following the elevation of Robert Stainthorpe (*qv*) to Alderman following the first elections to the County Council in 1889, Alexander joined the Council and was Hexham's representative there until his death. He was a county magistrate and a long-standing member of the Burial Board. He was a governor of the new Grammar School. William Alexander and his wife, Elizabeth are commemorated by part of the window at the east end of the Abbey.

The Rev. Henry Barker (1818-1899) (30) – Fishbourne Lecturer (appointed in 1862) and Rector of Hexham Abbey (appointed in 1863). Educated at Gonville and Caius College Cambridge, he was ordained by the Bishop of Lincoln in 1845. Prior to coming to Hexham he was perpetual curate of Morton (now continuous with Gainsborough) and East Stockwith, both villages in Lincolnshire. When in Hexham, he took a leading role in the restoration of the transepts and towers of the Abbey in 1870. He was much liked in the parish, taking an active part in public affairs. He was the first Chairman of the School Board, when it was formed in 1874. He resigned as Rector in 1898

Isaac Baty (1815-1888) (15) – Solicitor. He took a very active role in public affairs. He was Clerk to the Hexham Local Board of Health from 1863 and Secretary to the Burial Board from its inception until his death. For something

Fig. 6 (*across*) Plan of the original part of the Cemetery showing the location of the graves of those persons whose biographies are presented in this chapter. *See the top of page 28 for further information about the plan.*

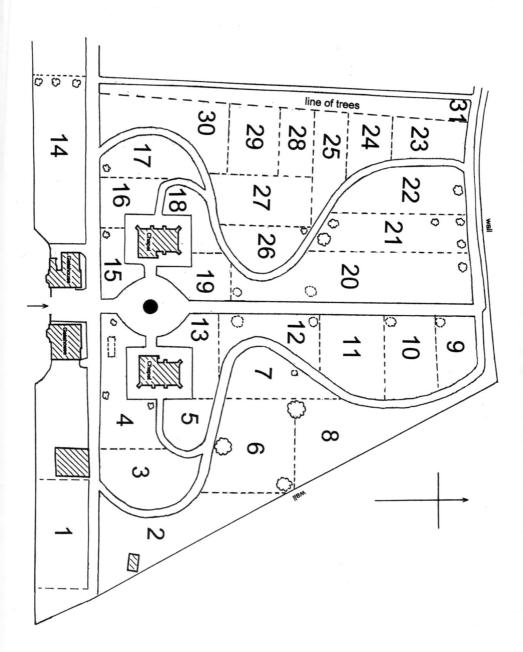

line of trees

wall

wall

Chapel

Chapel

Glasshouse

Glasshouse

14
31
30
29
28
25
24
23
22
21
20
17
16
18
15
19
13
12
11
10
9
7
8
6
5
4
3
2
1
27
26

30

like 30 years, he was elected annually as one of the people's churchwardens of the Abbey Church. He was auditor and solicitor to the Tindale Ward Savings Bank and Hexham Gas Company. He was the father of Isaac Baty, whose details follow.

Isaac Baty (1849-1894) (Lies in an unmarked grave in consecrated ground close to the chapel; his death is commemorated in the Cemetery by a memorial to him in the form of a replica of St Acca's cross, readily visible at the entrance) – Solicitor. He was in partnership with his father (*qv*) since 1872. He was educated at Gainford Academy, Darlington, after which he served his articles in Newcastle. Also in 1872, he was appointed Clerk of the Hexham Board of Guardians, carrying with it the post of Clerk of Hexham Rural Sanitary Authority and Superintendent Register of Births, Deaths and Marriages. He also became Clerk of the Bellingham Highway Board. In 1888, he succeeded to all the posts held by his father on his death, including election as a people's churchwarden. There were many other posts and positions that he held, a good number with various sporting clubs (he having been a keen sportsman in his youth); he seemed to attract posts and positions like a magnet. He was an energetic supporter of the Conservative Cause but an imprudent action in the 1892 General Election led to the result in the Hexham Division being declared void, resulting in the loss of his public appointments. Nevertheless, in 1893, he was presented with a £1000 note from members of the Conservative Party and after his death it was proposed to erect a memorial to him in front of the Abbey in the Market Place. There was considerable concern about this location; the memorial, referred to above, was eventually erected at the Cemetery.

George Bell (1811-1887) (4) – Chemist. He retired eventually a few years before his death in favour of his son-in-law, W. R. Riddle, who continued on the firm as Bell and Riddle. In conjunction with his brother, Mr Henry Bell (*qv*), he started the large business of tanners, skinners and manure manufacturers. He was a member of the Burial Board and for several years a member of the Local Board of Health. He was the first resident of Haining Croft.

George Hogarth Bell (1857-1905) (23) – Woolstapler and manure manufacturer. He was son of Henry Bell (*qv*) and one of the principal partners of Henry Bell & Sons. He was appointed a member of Local Board of Health in 1888, remaining a member until 1893. In 1889 he was elected to the School Board remaining on it to its dissolution in 1903, after which he was a manager of the Seal (as it was then spelt) Schools, now under local authority control. Canon Savage appointed Bell one of his Churchwardens. In 1903, after 27 years service with the

31

Volunteers he was made honorary lieutenant colonel. He played rugby for Northumberland. Bell is commemorated by part of the east window in Hexham Abbey; there is also an alabaster memorial to him in the south chancel aisle.

Henry Bell (1814-1875) (23) – Tanner, fellmonger, glove manufacturer and manure manufacturer. He was the brother of George Bell (*qv*). He acquired his knowledge of the tannery and wool trade from Smith Stobart the remains of whose tannery are still present in Tyne Green Road. The firm that Henry Bell and his brother started took his name. As a woolstapler, he was a supplier to the carpet manufacturers, Crossleys of Halifax.

Henry Bell (?-1920; 64) (23) – Woolstapler. He was the son of Henry Bell (*qv*). He and his brother George Hogarth Bell (*qv*) took over the firm when their father died. It became one of the leading firms in the country. It was responsible for the erection of the fine warehouse (now swimming bath) in Gilesgate. It also took over two other tanneries. Eventually, the woolstapling business became amalgamated with that of eight others under the name of Border Counties Wool Sales Ltd. In 1912, Henry Bell presented to the town the handsome bandstand in the Abbey Grounds.

Helen Rebecca Bickers-Stephenson (?-1924; ?) (19) – Voluntary worker. Helen Bickers-Stephenson, daughter of George Drew of Charles Street, Berkeley Square, London, had lived in Hexham since her marriage some forty years ago. She devoted much of her energies towards the Abbey, such as her leadership of the Mothers' Meeting for 29 years. In the 1914-18 War, she was treasurer for the two Voluntary Aid Detachment Hospitals at Cotfield and the Convalescent Home in Hextol Terrace. She was also a worker at the War Hospital Depot. After the war, she became a member of the Hexham War Memorial Hospital Committee and the Ambulance Committee.

William Bland (?-1902; 60) (17) – Builder. He was responsible for the houses in Shaftoe Leazes and other parts of the town. He purchased Windmill Hill and Kingsgate fields and was responsible for the stone houses and terraces that are now there, eventually living in one of them on Windmill Hill.

Rev. John G. Bowran (1869-1946) (2) – Primitive Methodist Minister. He was born in Gateshead and who came to Hexham in 1906 to the Hebbron Memorial Chapel in St Mary's Chare. He was the driving force for the building of the new (and fine) church at the corner of Beaumont Street. He is buried with his first wife who died of consumption shortly after they arrived in Hexham. He wrote several novels under the pen-name of 'Ramsey Guthrie' (Payne, 2002).

Joseph Catherall (1839-1881) (3) – Newspaper editor. He was born in Newcastle, becoming an apprentice to the *Newcastle Chronicle*, then, via a post in Bristol as reporter with the *Western Daily Press*, he arrived in Hexham to found, with others, in 1864, and edit the *Hexham Courant*. For a man of 25, he clearly had a deft touch and he founded well, since the paper is still flourishing today as a chronicler of and commentator on local events. Though a man with a frail constitution (he was to die of consumption) he played a highly significant and active role in the affairs of the town. Through the columns of the *Courant*, he fought long and hard for better sanitary conditions in Hexham. To paraphrase a quotation about him he was 'a knight-errant of his age; he forged a weapon out of public opinion that few evils could resist.' See Jennings (1998).

Matthew Charlton (?-1954; 66) (31) – Businessman. He was director of the former Hexham firm of M. Charlton and Sons, builders and plumbers merchants, and Past President of the Northern Federation of Roofing Contractors.

John Civil (?-1954; 93) (30) – Builder. He was the son of William Civil (*qv*), he obtained work as a joiner in Haltwhistle and Middlesborough and back in Hexham. Using the knowledge gained, he established his own building and contracting business, starting by building his own workshop in Hencotes. He built the Abbey Institute (now Community Centre) in Gilesgate, the Primitive Methodist Church at the corner of Beaumont Street and Battle Hill and the Methodist Churches at Lowgate and Warden. When he retired at 64, he built his own house at Fellside, hewing the stone himself from the near-by quarry. He represented Hencotes Ward on the Urban District Council from 1912 to 1924. When he died he was the last surviving member of Northumberland Volunteers who attended a review in Edinburgh before Queen Victoria.

William Civil (1819-1910) (30) – Builder. He had the distinction of living under six reigns and lived for 60 years at number one Holy Island, his residence when he died. He started work at the age of eight in Ridley's gloving factory, then becoming a tanner in the Hextol tannery; eventually he was a foreman supervising the making of the famous Hexham tans. In retirement he was engaged in market gardening.

Joseph (?-1898; 67) (29) and *William Darlington* (?-1903; 73) (30) – Builders. Together they built in Hexham, Henry Bell's Wool Warehouse in Gilesgate (now swimming baths), Lambton's (Lloyds TSB) Bank and villas in South Park. Outside Hexham, they built Prudhoe Church and manse and Farnley Grange near Corbridge. They were responsible for alterations and additions to Summerrods Rigg, Bank Head House and Loughbrow and carried out restorations at Langley and Haughton Castles.

John Dent (?-1932; 82) (4) – Millwright and pattern-maker in Hexham Iron Works. Dent came to Hexham 1865 to join Messrs Pattinson, Davison and Spencer, Hexham Iron Works and served the firm for 63 years. He started as an apprentice, eventually becoming head of the department. He was a prominent member of Hexham United Methodist Church. For over 60 years he was a preacher, and held many offices within the church. He had the unique distinction of having attended the annual school concert, which in the days of Tanners Row Chapel, was one of the chief events at Christmas. Dent was for fifteen years chairman of the Acomb and District Co-operative Society.

Thomas Dobson (?-1885; 71) (28) – Headmaster of Hexham Grammar School. Dobson himself was educated at the Grammar School. After school he went some time to live in France, where he became an English teacher. Returning to England, he joined Mr Thoroughgood's School near Totteridge as a mathematical master. It was here that he was able to improve himself mathematically such that he was admitted to St John's College, Cambridge to read the subject. Dobson graduated in 1819 as 17th Wrangler. On leaving the University, he was appointed mathematical master of the High School of Hobart, Tasmania. Returning to this country, he became mathematical master of the Royal Naval Schools Greenwich, then headmaster of H.M. Frigate 'Conway', moored in the Mersey. Webb, the first person to swim the channel, was one of his pupils. In 1862, Dobson came back to Hexham as the headmaster of the Grammar School, where he did much to improve its academic stature. He left Hexham in 1876 on his appointment as headmaster of the Marine School, South Shields, where he was in post when he died. He had a substantial reputation as a meteorologist, having lectured on the subject to such bodies as the Newcastle Literary and Philosophical Society and the British Association. See Jennings and Rossiter (1999).

Thomas Palliser Dods (1823-1891) (9) – Land agent. He was born in Belford, where his father was the Presbyterian Minister, coming to Tyneside around 1851 as tenant at the farm of Anick Grange. During his period as a farmer, he was very active in local affairs. He was chairman of the Board of Guardians (1863-1871) and Hexham Highways Board. He gave up farming to become a land agent and valuer, becoming agent for the Haughton Castle, Chipchase Castle and Heddon and Langley Castle estates. He was responsible, in the late 1870s, for a valuation of Hexham Township for rateable purposes.

Thomas Ellis (?-1920; 74) (22) – Painter and glazier. Thomas was the only son of William Ellis, who was also painter and glazier, and was for a short time a member of the Local Board of Health. Thomas followed his father into the business and prospered, as seen by the shop (and firm) still bearing his name in Beaumont Street, and similarly became a member of the Local Board of Health from 1881-84. Thomas was a very active member of Hexham Mechanics' Institute, which eventually rented a room in his building at the top of Hallstile Bank and also a churchwarden at the time of the rebuilding of the nave of the Abbey.

Joseph Fairless (1789-1873) (30) – Numismatist and antiquarian. Fairless, born in Corbridge, spent most of his life in Hexham, where he was a house painter. He was a guardian of the poor, a governor of the Royal Grammar School and was officially connected with the Free (Subscription) School, was several times elected as churchwarden and on the managing committee of the Savings' Bank. But Fairless's claim to fame was as numismatist, stimulated by the finding by a grave-digger in 1832 of a bucket containing about 8000 Saxon stycas, small copper coins current in Northumbria in the 9th century. He took a major role in dating and deciphering the inscriptions on the coins. He wrote an excellent guide to the Abbey. He enjoyed the respect and friendship of other antiquarians throughout the country such as Dr Bruce and was a personal friend of the Earl of Northumberland. His gravestone is notable for bearing a fine photograph (Fig. 7). Three windows in east side of the north transept of Hexham Abbey commemorate Joseph Fairless. See Anon. (1913*a*).

William Fell (?-1903; 56) (3) – Nurseryman. Prior to coming to Hexham, Fell had been connected for over fourteen years with the firm of Little and Ballantyne of Carlisle, where he had been head of the seed department. In 1879, Fell took over the nursery business of the recently deceased Ralph Robson. Two years later, Fell was joined by William Milne and they continued in partnership until 1901, when the firm became a limited liability company. It was to become

---

Fig. 7 (*across*) The gravestone of Joseph Fairless showing the fine photograph of him. There are only a handful of photographs on gravestones in Hexham Cemetery. Now one wishes there were more on those erected in the 19th century, for we have too few photographs of notable Hexhamonians from this period.

one of the best nurseries in the country, also having business overseas, including the continent, USA and the colonies. The firm was to hold a Royal Warrant and was based on the Wentworth nurseries, which took up the area now covered by the car park, Safeway's supermarket and the sports facilities.

John Gibson FSA (?-1936; 65) (25) – Optician, archaeologist and antiquarian. Son of John Pattinson Gibson (*qv*), like him he was a fine photographer. He, through his lecturing and writing did much to make known to a wider audience the richness of the archaeology and history of the northeast. He ran the pharmacy in Fore Street, the furnishings and contents of which are now in the Science Museum in London. In 1908, as a consequence of Gibson being freeman and fellow of the Worshipful Company of Spectacle-makers (established by Royal Charter in 1629) the freedom of the City of London was conferred upon him. He was President of the Society of Chemist-Opticians and fellow of both the Chemical Society of London and the Institute of Ophthalmic Opticians.

John Pattinson Gibson FRPS, FSA (1838-1912) (25) – Famous as a photographer and archaeologist. Educated at the Queen Elizabeth and Newcastle Grammar Schools, he served his time as a chemist and druggist with his father. Following a period in Newcastle, he took over his father's shop when he died. In 1856, he took up photography, which he pursued with such diligence that, in ten years, he had earned an international reputation, winning prizes in open competition in such places as London, Melbourne, Paris, New York, Berlin, Chicago and Vienna. After giving up exhibition work in 1891, he became deeply involved in archaeological research, often helping to supervise excavations, particularly on Roman sites in the area. He was a highly esteemed lecturer, supported by his incomparable slides. He made a major contribution to the *Northumberland County History* through the provision of photographs for the volumes. He was an enthusiastic Volunteer, rising to the rank of Major. See Anon (1913*b*) and Neilson (1912).

Frank Gibb Grant (1850-1918) (4) – Owner of the Tynedale Hydropathic Establishment in Hexham. He was born just south of Forres in Scotland. He came to prominence in the hydropathic movement as manager of Conishead Priory Hydropathic Mansion near Ulverston in what is now Cumbria. When the Tynedale Hydropathic ran into financial problems, it was leased to a Scottish consortium headed by Frank Grant and a John McPherson. Soon, Grant, because of his experience of the sector, bought the entire business for himself and spent £30,000 on enhancing the building. A notable enhancement was the addition of the Winter Gardens in 1906. While he was manager, the Hydro was 'one of the most attractive and popular health resorts in the North of England'. Grant was from 1905 a member of the Hexham Urban District Council for seven years. For twenty-six years he was a member of the Board of Guardians. He was a keen huntsman. See Durie (2002).

John Guthrie (?-1890; 53) (17) – Painter and decorator. He resided in the Sun Inn, Fore Street, which he owned along with the Criterion and Tanner's Arms Inn. At the time of his death he had been a member of the Local Board of Health for ten years, being Chairman from 1884-7. He was a keen pigeon fancier, his birds having taken prizes at many of the leading exhibitions in the country.

William Harrison (?-1898; 66) (30) – Watchmaker and Jeweller. He was member of a line of watchmakers, his father being Francis Harrison, who set up his business in the town in 1824. William's sons, buried in the same plot, continued on the tradition.

Charles Head (?-1868; 74) (30) – Solicitor. He was educated at the Grammar School and, because his home was distant from Hexham – his father was Vicar of Chollerton – was a boarder during the whole of his school career. On leaving, he became articled to John Bell, attorney and bailiff of the Manor, a quixotic person who was an intimate friend of William Cobbett, whose opinions persuaded Bell to plant Indian corn outside his mansion at the Dene. Head took a very active role in the running of the Town. He was a driving force for the building of the Town Hall and Corn Exchange (now the Queen's Hall). In spite of lack of success in the elections of 1854 and 1862, he was elected in 1863 to the Local Board of Health, becoming Chairman for three years in 1866. He did much to help the movement for a better water supply and sewage system succeed. He was one of the public-spirited gentlemen who took over the lease of the Seal and opened it to the public for the whole year, when previously it had only been open during the winter months. A window in Hexham Abbey commemorates Charles Head and his wife, Elizabeth.

J. Oswald Head (?-1914; 85) – Solicitor. Son of Charles Head (*qv*), Oswald Head took a prominent role in the life of the Hexham. He was one of the managers of the local branch of the Cumberland Union Bank and a trustee of the Tindale Ward Savings Bank and he was a general commissioner of Income Tax. He was a keen tennis player and was vice-president of the Tynedale Athletic Association. Oswald Head played a prominent role in the affairs of the Abbey, being a churchwarden. He was actively involved in the restoration of the east end which commenced in 1858. Though his Hexham home was Hackwood, it

38

seems he was increasingly absent from Hexham, most probably living in Eastbourne.

Elizabeth Hebbron (1803-1863; 60) – Wife of Henry Hebbron (*qv*), whom she married in 1831. The inscription on her grave says 'she was a humble, zealous and useful Christian'. She died in Yorkshire at Potto, just south of Middlesborough, close to the North York Moors. One of her brothers was Errington Ridley (*qv*), who wrote a book about her Christian approach to life and death, another was John Ridley, glove manufacturer, 'an uncompromising friend of civil and religious liberty'. Her portrait is shown in Fig. 8.

Henry Hebbron (?-1860; 54) – Primitive Methodist Minister. Born in Potto on a small estate farmed by his father, 'thirty-five years were spent in the faithful and successful ministry of the Gospel'. Hebbron Chapel, the building of which is still present in St Mary's Chare, was built as a memorial to him.

George Hedley (?-1916; 79) (29) – Joiner, cabinet maker and furniture dealer in St Mary's Chare (the shop is still there). He was a member of the Local Board of Health from 1880 until its demise in 1894. He played a not inconsiderable part in moving the attitude of the Board towards change. He was chairman of the Hexham Corn Exchange and Public Buildings Company.

Cuthbert James Herdman (?-1920; 63) (16) – Builder. He was the son of an engineer, living in Wall. He came to Hexham and succeeded to the business of his uncle, the builder Edward Herdman. His firm erected the convalescent home of the Cathedral Nurse and Loan Society in Hextol Terrace and the London and Midland (now HSBC) Bank at the end of Fore Street. He was a lessee of Darney Quarry near Woodburn famous for its fine stone, much of it being used in the new nave of the Abbey and extensively used for buildings in Newcastle. Fig. 9 (*see page 41*) shows the certificate for Herdman's exclusive Right of Burial in Grave Space 331 in the Cemetery.

Kingsley W. D. Hodgson (?-1944; 38) (31) – School sports master. He was killed, when a Major in the Home Guard, as the result of an exercise to detonate mines that went sadly wrong. At the time of his death he was games master at the Grammar School. Educated at St John's School, Leatherhead and Durham

---

Fig. 8 (*across*) Portrait of Elizabeth Hebbron (from a photograph?) that forms the frontispiece of the book about her by Errington Ridley (1863) and referred to above (reproduced by courtesy of Newcastle City Library).

W. DICKES SC.

Yrs truly & affectionately
Eliza Hebbron

No. *532*

Hexham Burial Board.

We, the Burial Board for the Township of HEXHAM, in the County of NORTHUMBERLAND, in consideration of the sum of *Two*

pounds

paid to us by *Cuthbert James Herdman*

of *Hexham* in the County of *North*

the receipt whereof is hereby acknowledged, Do, by virtue of the powers vested in us by the Acts 15 & 16 Victoria, cap. 85, and 16 & 17 Victoria, cap. 134, hereby grant unto the aforesaid

Cuthbert James Herdman the exclusive Right of

Burial in the Grave Space No. *331* in section *C* of the ———— consecrated part of the Burial Ground provided under the said Acts, and the other Acts incorporated therewith, by the BURIAL BOARD aforesaid, To Hold the same to the said

Cuthbert James Herdman his heirs and assigns, for ever, for the purpose of Burial, subject nevertheless to the payment of such fees or sums as are reserved by the said Acts, or any of them, or by the said BURIAL BOARD, and also subject to the regulations now in force, or which may hereafter be issued with regard to Interments in the said Burial Ground, by Her Majesty's Secretary of State, or by the said BURIAL BOARD, or any other competent authority.

Given under our Hands and under the Seal of the BURIAL BOARD for the Township of HEXHAM, in the County of NORTHUMBER-LAND, this *Sixth* day of *February* One thousand eight hundred and ninety————

L.S.

John W. Robson } Members of
William ———— } the said
Burial Board.

Thos. W. ———— Clerk to the Board.

41

University, Hodgson was one of the best-known rugby footballers in the North, having the unique experience of having captained Northumberland against Cheshire when first selected for the County side in October 1933, continuing as captain until 1936. He had previously played for Durham and Yorkshire. He led the Tynedale Club (then at Hexham) to victory in the Northumberland Senior Cup for four successive seasons, starting in 1932-3.

William Iveson (?-1922; 70) (10) – Auctioneer. He was born near Hawes in Wensleydale. He joined his father who had an extensive business in the sale of fat cattle and horses at Manchester and Wakefield markets and who regularly visited Northumberland. It was his father who suggested that William should settle in the county. He started at Dilston High Town in 1875 but went to Aydon White House, eventually settling in Hexham in Tynedale House in 1885. In 1879, with his brother, he took a controlling interest in the auction mart of William Cook and Co. in Hexham. When Cook died, the business became known as the Hexham Auction Mart Co. It became one of the most successful and best managed marts in the country. The Bellingham mart came under the control of the company. Iveson was known as an eloquent preacher on the Methodist circuit.

Daniel Jackson (1838-1911) (30) – Doctor. He was born in Cambuslang, Lanarkshire and educated at Glasgow Eastern Academy and Glasgow University, graduating with M.D. in 1862. He became the first Medical Officer of Health for Hexham in 1873. For the sanitary development of the town it proved to be an inspired choice. Jackson was fearless in his condemnation of unsanitary practices and was fiercely persistent in his dealings with the Board in trying to get changes brought about. He retired from his post in 1911 to be succeeded by his son who in his own distinguished manner built on his father's approach to public health matters.

Charles Knight (?-1965; 82) (3) – Proprietor of the bakery firm of B. Knight and Son, founded by his grandmother. He was four times chairman of the Urban District Council, as well as being for 23 years Chairman of the Hexham and District National Savings Committee. He was a County Councillor. He was also chairman of the Hexham Entertainments Company, responsible for the Queen's Hall (when it contained a cinema and ballroom) and the Forum Cinema. Knight

---

Fig. 9 (*across*) A copy of the certificate for Cuthbert Herdman's exclusive 'Right of Burial in Grave Space 331' (reproduced by kind permission of Mrs Joyce Stockdale).

was a keen bowler, playing for Northumberland on several occasions; in 1938 he was made President of the Northumberland Bowling Association.

Herbert Lees (?-1944; 82) (3) – Manager, Hexham Gas Company. He was born in the West Riding of Yorkshire. In 1882, he went to the Carlisle council to serve his articles as a gas engineer. After serving his articles, he went to Widnes Corporation Gas Works in 1886. In March 1991, he came to Hexham as Secretary and manager of the Gas Works. He was clearly highly respected in his profession, becoming President of the North of England Gas Managers'Association in 1895 and 1927. For twelve years he was member of the Urban District Council. He was a manager of the Council Schools, a governor of the Grammar School and chairman of the local branch of the League of Nations Association. Lees was member of the Wesleyan communion and a staunch supporter of the Trinity Church. He had held every office in the Church open to a layman and was a member of the Synod.

Andrew Little (?-1912; 77) (4) – Miller. He was a native of Stapleton, to the west of Bewcastle, serving his apprenticeship as a miller in Cummertrees Mill near Annan. He commenced business with his father at Chainleyford Mill, near Bardon Mill, moving to Nunwick Mill, near Simonburn and then Wood Hall Mill at Haydon Bridge. About 1868, he went into partnership with his brother taking over the Allendale Mill. Realising that more modern methods were necessary and that a more central location was needed if the firm was to expand, they opened the large mill (which is still present, though now converted into apartments) in Priestpopple in 1884 in the building previously owned by the Northumberland Brewery. The machinery installed was the most up-to-date available and was only selected after the two brothers had visited mills in this and other countries. The establishment of the new mill in Hexham, based on the rolling process, proved a most successful venture such that the firm became a limited company in 1911.

Lewis Chalmers Lockhart (1848-1925) (30) – Solicitor. When he died he was acclaimed one of 'Hexham's most distinguished citizens'. A native of the town, he was educated at the Grammar School after which he joined the business of John Bell, who was bailiff of the Manors of Hexham and of Anick Grange. Bell took Charles Head (*qv*) into partnership. In 1868, following the deaths of Bell and then Head, Lockhart took over the running of the firm, taking his brother H. F. Lockhart into partnership in 1881. In 1916, the firm was taken over by the firm of solicitors, Clayton and Gibson of Newcastle. Not only was Lockhart a highly industrious legal advisor, taking a firm line on behalf of his clients, but also, as practitioner, he was involved on many outside bodies He was much involved in educational matters, being a member of the Hexham School Board, continuing as a manager of the Seal (as it was then spelt) Schools. He was a governor of Queen Elizabeth Grammar School and largely instrumental in the erection of the then new Building at Fellside in 1910. He was secretary of the Allenheads and Plashetts and Tynehead School Boards He was chairman of the Gas Board, clerk to and director of the Town Hall and Public Buildings Co., a trustee of the Tindale Ward Savings bank, a governor of Hexham Dispensary, and treasurer of the Hexham Branch of the Cathedral and Loan Society. In 1864 he joined the ranks of the Hexham Company of the 2nd Northumberland Rifle Volunteer Corps and retired in 1910 as Commanding Officer, with the rank of colonel, of the 4th Battalion Northumberland Fusiliers. He was a noted marksman, being three times in the last stage of the Queen's Prize at Wimbledon, the forerunner of Bisley. He was a very active churchwarden under Canon Barker (*qv*). Lewis Lockhart lived in the latter part of his life at Summmerrods Rigg. See Jennings (2001).

The Rev. John E. McVitie (?-1925; 58) (4) – Minister of the Hexham Presbyterian Church. He was a native of Maryport in Cumbria. He was educated at the Edinburgh University and the Theological College of the English Presbyterian Church in London. After being an assistant at Regent Square Church, Camden, he came to Hexham in 1900. He was the first minister to be ordained in the Presbyterian Church that was then in Battle Hill. He was much liked by his congregation. He took an active part in public affairs, in particular he was a member of the Board of Guardians, becoming Chairman the year before he died and played an important role in the running of the War Memorial Hospital. He was a staunch supporter of the temperance movement and fought what was, in the end, a losing battle against the opening of cinemas on Sunday. As the *Courant* put it 'there was a strain of the old Presbyters in Mr McVitie, though it rarely obtruded itself......it was mellowed to a charming graciousness by a tolerant and kindly nature'.

Irwin Murray (?-1907; 72) (10) – Gentleman. Murray came to Hexham around 1860. For twenty years he kept dining rooms in Fore Street, in which business he was so successful that he was able to retire. Nevertheless he took an active interest in public life. He was a member of Hexham Urban District Council from 1898 until his death.

John Nicholson (1815-1887) (28) – Sometime doctor. In his early life he was a pupil of Philip Jefferson, surgeon, Hall Stile Bank. He then went to Edinburgh

University where he had a distinguished student career, being awarded the gold medal for highest proficiency in all branches of medicine. He studied at Guys Hospital and Paris. After a very successful career as a surgeon, he retired around 1865. On the formation of the Hexham Rifle Volunteers, Nicholson enrolled as surgeon in 1860. He became eventually commanding officer of what had then become A Company of the 1st Volunteer Battalion Northumberland Fusiliers. In 1881, he retired with the honorary rank of Lieutenant Colonel. In 1871, he was elected chairman of the Board of Guardians, President of the then influential Farmers' Club and churchwarden during the restoration of the chancel of the Abbey Church in the period 1858-60, when the east end was rebuilt.

John Harbottle Nicholson (?-1941; 81) (28) – Son of John Nicholson (*qv*). In 1930, he retired after 37 years in the post of Clerk Hexham Board of Guardians. This body also undertook the role of the Hexham Rural Sanitary Authority, for which Nicholson was also Clerk. This latter organisation was complex comprising of 57 parishes, some with more autonomy than others with respect to management of their highways. In 1894, the Authority became the Hexham Rural District Council. Nicholson played cricket for Tynedale and was one of the leading spirits in the formation of the Tynedale Athletic Association.

William Pattinson (?-1937; 75) (31) – Chemist. Born in Haltwhistle, Pattinson served his apprenticeship as a chemist with Bell and Riddle. During that period he was one of the key members of Tynedale Rugby Club, playing in the three quarters and noted for his fearless tackling. He was in the Northumberland team on many occasions. In order to gain more experience in his profession Pattinson spent time in London and Bath, where he played rugby for Bath and Somerset. On his return to Hexham in 1898, he established a chemist's business in Cattle Market. He continued his rugby for Tynedale and was selected for an England trial but was unable to play because of business commitments. He was a member of the Urban District Council from 1908 to 1915. In 1925 he became Chairman of the Hexham Gas Company.

Edward Pruddah (?-1879; 33) (26) – Bookseller and printer. He is notable for starting the *Hexham Herald* in 1867. That newspaper, of Conservative outlook was to prove during the remaining years of the 19th century an important foil to the Liberal *Courant*. However, after three years, Pruddah found that the paper did not realise his expectations and he sold it to other proprietors, confining his attention on his printing and bookselling business. At the time of his death, due to excessive alcohol consumption, there had been an Edward Pruddah in Hexham during the previous 200 years.

William Pruddah (?-1912; 65) (26) – Solicitor. He was the son of William Pruddah, chemist in Fore Street. He served his articles as a solicitor with Messrs Chartres and Youll of Newcastle. After being admitted as a solicitor in 1874, he commenced work in Hexham and soon made a name for himself in the courts. In 1893, he succeeded Isaac Baty (*qv*) as Clerk of the Urban District Council, resigning in 1908, after unwarranted slurs on his integrity by a Councillor. In 1886, he became a member of the School Board, continuing as manager of the Hexham Council Schools. In 1896, he became Superintendent Registrar of Births Marriages and Deaths He was a very active supporter of the Mechanics' Institute.

Robert Richardson (?-1922; 63) (7) – Managing director of shoe dealers. He was born at Halton-le-Gate and went to Haltwhistle when he was fifteen. There he apprenticed himself to a clog-maker, eventually setting up in business in the town. About 1892, he came to Hexham as manager for Messrs Scott and Son, boot and shoe dealers in Fore Street, becoming managing director when the firm became a limited liability company. In 1915, he became a member of the Urban District Council, becoming Chairman in 1920. It was during his term of office that the Council's first housing scheme, at Peth Head, was inaugurated, Richardson cutting the first sod. He was an ardent Methodist, playing a significant role in the activities of Trinity Church and, when it was opened, he and a colleague formed the church's choir.

Errington Ridley (1801-1880) (5) – Tanner. The *Hexham Courant* wrote about him, on his death as follows: 'Without claiming too much for him, it may with truth be said that his hand was in almost every good and philanthropic movement for many years. He took a warm interest in the old reading room, the temperance cause, and in all missionary efforts, particularly in branches locally represented, and gave a good deal to charity in a quiet way. Amongst what we might call his eccentricities, was his determined antipathy to tobacco smoking and other indulgencies of a kindred nature. Mr Ridley had been connected, as a shareholder, with the Hexham and Allendale Railway from the commencement, and zealously opposed any steps in its management likely to result in Sunday traffic.' Although he died at Burswell House, for business reasons he resided in Newcastle for many years. He was actively involved in the Gilesgate School. A memoir (Anon, 1930) speaks about the early days of the institution when the teachers 'had to encounter great difficulties with the untamed children they had gathered in. Stand-up fights were not uncommon and simultaneous rushes to the door had to be guarded against.' Eventually more normal conditions prevailed. The memoir also goes on to say 'in his old age, Mr Ridley took a deep interest in many young men who had removed from Hexham and Newcastle, to whom he sent religious books and with whom he maintained a correspondence. To reduce the cost of postage, he had the margins cut off, so that the books were rendered very unsightly, and I believe he afterwards found out that he had saved nothing by this disfigurement. His intentions were good, if methods were peculiar, and his little weaknesses were not minimised by his fellow townsmen.'

John Ridley (1817-1892) (5) – Wool-stapler, tanner and manure manufacturer. He was a member of the Board of Guardians and a manager of the Seal Subscription School and for fifteen years (1864-76 & 1878-81) a member of the Local Board of Health, being one of those members who fought for sanitary reform against the intransigence and laissez-fair stance of the majority. Towards the end of Ridley's term of office the Board had swung to his way of thinking and before he died progress was being made not only towards reducing the death rate but also towards raising Hexham to a position of a popular health resort. Ridley was closely associated with the Gilesgate Sunday School, being one of its founders and also its superintendent for a number of years. It was very successful, outgrowing the building in Tanners' Row and moving to the Subscription School on the Seal. Ridley originated the annual trip, by special train, to Tynemouth that, at the time of his death, had run for 49 years. As a member of the Wild Birds' Association he urged children to treat animals kindly and not to rob birds' nests. He strongly supported the Temperance Movement. He was also part of a group of likeminded men and women who did much to try to improve the living conditions of the poor at the bottom of Gilesgate. Ridley was not only an active member of the Congregational Church but he was also a strong supporter of the Salvation Army. He was married to the sister of William Robb (*qv*).

William Ritson (1811-1893) (25) – Railway contractor. He was born at Mugglewick Park, County Durham. He started a life as a businessman at the infancy of the railways and carried out many contracts in the making of railways. He was responsible for the section of the Newcastle and Carlisle Railway between Hexham and Bardon Mill. From there he went to Northallerton and thence to Dumfries where he carried out a contract near there. He spent eleven years in Wales where the contracts included the making of the Vale of Neath Railway. He returned to Scotland in 1860, he built eight miles of the North British Railway from Riccarton to Shankend, including the Whitrope tunnel. His final construction work was the making of the Hexham and Allendale Railway. He retired to a mansion that he built at Woodley Field.

James Thomas Robb (?- 1927; 73) (13) – Businessman and civic leader. Son of William Robb (*qv*), who established the business of W. Robb and Son Ltd., he worked with his father in the running of the firm. From the time that James Robb became associated with the firm, it expanded almost continuously. When it moved from its then premises in Hall Gate to the north end of Fore Street, James Robb took sole charge of the firm. There were to be further moves, such that when Robb died, the firm was occupying two large premises at the end of Fore Street, one on the west side, occupying the site of Mackay's, and the other on the east side, on the site of the White Hart Inn, being the forerunner of the present store. James Robb, like his father played a major role in the life of the town. He was elected to the Local Board of Health in 1882. He became Chairman in 1887. It was under his chairmanship that the town obtained excellent water from Ladle Wells replacing the totally inadequate supply close to the town. On the inception of the Urban District Council in 1894, he did not stand immediately for election to that body. However he returned to the hustings in 1904 and was elected again to the Urban District Council, becoming Chairman for the period 1907-13. Then he fought through the purchase of the Abbey Grounds, against the faint hearts of many on the Council. In 1910, he became a County Councillor. He was on many public bodies but the one for which he is remembered was the Hexham War Memorial Hospital Committee of which he was chairman. He was one of the earliest advocates of a hospital as War Memorial and presided over the proceedings when Prince Henry opened the building and unveiled the War Memorial in the Abbey Grounds in 1921. As a thanksgiving for the safe return of three sons from the First World War, he presented the Georgian Arch that stands at the Beaumont Street entrance to the Abbey Grounds and on which are bronze tablets that are a memorial to 4th Battalion Northumberland Fusiliers. Robb was keen golfer and was one of the promoters of the first club on Tyne Green and also of the Club that is now at The Spital. He was actively associated with the formation of the Tynedale Athletics Association.

Ralph Henry Robb (?-1927; 73) (13) – Sportsman. Known as Harry, he was the youngest son of William Robb (*qv*) at the time of his death regarded 'as probably the best all-round athlete Hexham has ever produced.' He was associated particularly with Tynedale Rugby Club, playing in the first match (against Elswick) after the club's formation in the autumn of 1876. He was twice President of the Club. He was able to play anywhere on the field. However, his rugby reputation was based on his skill and tenacious tackling as a full back and it was in this position that he played for Northumberland for several seasons. One of the earliest members of Hexham Cricket Club, as with rugby, representing his county in the sport. He was for many years one of Hexham's best all-round players. In particular, he was a fast and destructive bowler. He was able to throw a cricket ball a tremendous distance. On the athletics track he was a fine hurdler and middle distance runner. He was a keen golfer and, latterly in his life an enthusiastic bowler. In his early years, Robb was associated with the firm of John Ridley (*qv*) and Son, wool merchants and fellmongers. Later, he became a member of his father's firm.

William Robb (?-1892; 76) (13) – Draper. Some idea of the esteem with which Robb was held by his contemporaries can be judged by the fact that his obituary in the *Courant*, the longest on record, filled half a page and then without a customary description of the funeral which was associated with many obituaries. At the age of four, he arrived from Kirriemuir in Scotland with his father, who was to start in business as a draper in Fore Street. Robb went to a school in Hencotes run by the Rev. George Bell, who taught him Greek, Hebrew and Latin. After he joined his father's business, undertaking the duties of traveller, covering an wide area (on foot) that included Bellingham, Kirkheaton, Belsay and Angerton. On the death of his father, Robb took over the business that was then in Hall Gates. In 1873, he took his son, James into partnership. Four years later they moved to Beaumont Street and then in 1891 they moved again to a new building adapted to modern requirements at the north end of Fore Street. William Robb will always be associated with sanitary reform. He was amongst the first of the agitators for a better water supply and sewage system. In spite of the damning 1853 Government Report that followed that agitation, the first election for the Local Board of Health led to a membership that was against such reform. But eventually, in the 1860s, the 'clean party' triumphed over the 'dirty party', Robb himself becoming elected in 1863. The following year, Robb was one of those who initiated the construction of a new water supply. Subsequent years saw improvements in the sewage system. He was Chairman of the Board from 1869-73. He was a driving force for the acquisition of Tyne Green by the Board, though the negotiations started in 1866 it was 1887 before there was a successful outcome. Robb was clearly a man of integrity. He resigned from the Board in 1876, because, although he was acting in good faith, he found he had wrongly negotiated on behalf of the Board for some land on which it was planned to build a slaughterhouse. In similar manner, he wrote privately in 1877 to the Local Government Board about the failure of the Local Board to fulfil its sanitary obligations, urging that it not be disbanded and power given to the

Fig. 10 (*across*) Part of the portrait of William Robb by John Charlton that was presented to the Hexham Urban District Council by Robb's three sons in 1912 (reproduced by kind permission of Tynedale Council).

Hexham Rural Sanitary Authority. Robb was an ardent supporter of education, being a manager of the Subscription School when it was at the top of Eastgate and subsequently on the Seal, a member of the School Board and a very active supporter of the Mechanics' Institute. He joined colleagues, such as John Ridley (*qv*) in starting the Gilesgate Sunday School. He was a major force in the Methodist Church in the area, much in demand as a preacher. He was also a powerful speaker for the temperance movement. He wrote many articles. However, the most notable item of his literary output is *Hexham Fifty Years Ago*, which presents a vivid picture of social life within the town in the 1840s. His portrait is shown in Fig. 10 (*see page 50*).

Charles Robson (1870-1961) (26) – Draper. Son of Henry Robson (*qv*) he was apprenticed to the firm of Bainbridge's in Newcastle. In 1911, he started his own business ('The Corner Shop') in Hexham, running it until 1945. He was a member of the Board of Guardians and he was a founder member of the Hexham Cage Bird Society.

Edward W. Robson (1869-1944) (26) – Commercial traveller. Son of Henry Robson (*qv*), he travelled on behalf of his brother Charles (*qv*). He was a sidesman and bellringer in the Abbey and secretary of Hexham Unionist Club. He was very active in horticultural circles, being at one time secretary of Hexham Flower Show, when it was held in the Abbey Grounds, and was one of the founders of Hexham Horticultural Society.

Henry Robson (1826-1914) (26) – Superintendent of the Cemetery. Robson was the first superintendent (*see chapter on the history of the Cemetery*), remaining superintendent for 41 years. Under his regime the number of interments reached over 4,600. Prior to coming to Hexham, he was in the employment of Mr Hewitson of Elswick Hall. He married into the Harrison Family (*qv*).

Hugh Robson (1859-1938) (19) – Confectionary businessman. Son of Henry Robson (*qv*), he started career working with his uncle John Young, who ran a provision merchant's shop in the Market Place. He was a prominent member of Hexham Amateur Rowing Club. Eventually, he went to South Shields where he established a confectionary business that became very successful with eleven shops and 50 staff.

James Robson (1857-1919) (26) – Draper. Son of Henry Robson (*qv*), he established, around 1884, a business in what used to be the Wigton Clothing

Factory in Jubilee Buildings. He was known as 'Jubilee Jimmy'. He was a keen member of the Elvaston Bowling Club, dying prior to a match with a team from Newcastle, which he had got together. He was a manager of the Presbyterian Church.

John W. Robson (?-1928; 84) (26) – Nurseryman. He had extensive nurseries at the bottom of Hall Stile Bank, on Causey Hill and, until the land was sold for building purposes, at the Leazes He was a recognised authority on forest trees, conifers and shrubs. He had a high reputation for rose trees which he grew on Causey Hill. He was a founder member of the English Arboricultural Society, some of the formation meetings being held at his house. He was a member of the Burial Board.

Robert Robson (?-1907; 58) (23) – For 33 years he was Parish Clerk and Verger of the Abbey. He had also been a choirboy and was one of the bell-ringers. He took a keen interest in the archaeology and architecture of the Abbey. When clearing out the accumulated earth from the floor of the crypt, he found some pieces of 13th-century glass and various other artefacts.

Thomas Rowell (1842-1914) (4) – Actuary. He joined the United Free Church, the forerunner of West End Methodist Church. Born in Newcastle, when a young man, becoming a local preacher, chapel trustee and circuit steward. He was Actuary of the Tindale Ward Savings Bank, Registrar of Births and Deaths and treasurer to Hexham Soup Kitchen

Edward Shield (?-1941; 92) (3) – Director of the firm of W. A. Temperley Co. Ltd, Corn and Agricultural Merchants, Newcastle and Hexham. He joined the staff in 1869, becoming a partner in 1901. He was a regular visitor to all the local marts and could remember William Cook's mart when it was situated in Beaumont Street. He was present at the inaugural meeting of Tynedale Rugby Club, when he was elected treasurer. When he died was the oldest member of Hexham Cricket Club, Hexham Golf Club and the Elvaston Bowling Club. He represented England against Ireland at bowls and had played every county in the country. Not surprisingly, he earned the title of Hexham's Grand Old Man of sport.

Robert Bolam Short (1842-1930) (12) – Railway worker. He was a native of Hexham. At the age of fourteen, he was hired as a farm servant near Prudhoe. Later he worked at Medomsley and other places. Before becoming a cartman for Thomas Bullman, the noted local mason, he had the distinction of leading the first batch of stone from Oakwood Quarry for the erection of the Town Hall buildings. He then worked for the Local Board of Health as a cartman. Finally he joined the North Eastern Railway Company, in the capacity as rolleyman in which capacity he was with Company for 40 years. A rolley is a trolly without sides but we also know from photographs that Short also acted as a cartman for the Railway Company. He made local history in 1892 when he stood as the working man's representative for election to the Local Board of Health and, although his candidature was not taken seriously, he headed the poll with 996 vote – 331 votes more than the next successful candidate. Subsequently, he was elected to the Urban District Council when it succeeded the Local Board of Health, remaining a member until 1901. He did much to improve the Fire Brigade.

Matthew Smith (1806-1886) (30) – Farmer. He was Chairman of the Local Board of Health from its inception in 1854 until 1866, when Charles Head (*qv*) replaced him. He had a *laissez faire* attitude to the implementation of sanitary reform. Even while he was chairman, he was accused by one of his tenants of not only failing to clear the yard of the property of human excrement but of using it as a store of manure to be eventually used on his land. Eventually, in 1877, after several years of complaints, the magistrates fined him over the unsanitary state of two of his properties in the town. He benefited from the provision of the new water supply in 1864, since he was able to sell to the Local Board of Health the land on which the reservoir was built. Smith was a member of the Board of Guardians for over forty years. He seems to have been an effective farmer; he kept bulls that won prizes a different local cattle shows. He lived at Loughbrow.

Edward Snowball (?-1923; 82) (9) – Builder. He was associated with the erection of some of Hexham's most notable buildings – the offices of the *Hexham Courant*, the Presbyterian Church that used to be in Battle Hill, the North Eastern Bank in Beaumont Street (now the Conservative Club), Lambton's Bank (now Lloyds TSB), the new premises for Robbs at the south end of Fore Street (now Mackay's), Loughbrow House and Woodley Field. Since the age of nineteen, he was an active preacher on the Methodist circuit, often walking long distances to keep his preaching appointment. He was elected to the Local Board of Health in 1883 and was one of the new forward-thinking members who helped to procure the water supply from Ladle Wells. He was a member of the Board of Guardians and a member of the Burial Board.

Robert Stainthorpe (?- 1913; 87) (12) – Parliamentary Registration Agent. He is notable for his contribution to local government affairs. He began his public career in 1880 when he was elected to the School Board of which he was a member of upwards of twenty years. He succeeded Canon Barker (*qv*) to the chairmanship of the Board. In 1882, he was elected to the Board of Health and he sat on it and the successor authority, the Urban District Council, continuously until he retired in 1904. He was elected Chairman of the Council in 1899. He was a forceful person who he knew his own mind. Sometimes he could be wrong but, in general, he was a forward-looking person. He was on the committee under whose auspices water from Ladle Wells was brought to Hexham. Notable was his proposal that there should be a pipeline from the supply to the reservoir across to Causey Hill and thence to the Allendale Road, making it easier to supply the buildings in the area, such as the Hydro, allowing a suitable pressure to be maintained. He was a strong supporter of technical education. His tenacity of purpose helped in the fight to obtain possession of Tyne Green for the Local Board. He was elected to the County Council when it was established in 1888 and was amongst the first batch of councillors to be appointed an alderman. His portrait is shown in Fig. 11 (*see page 56*).

Thomas Gardner Stainthorpe (1816-1899; 83) (12) – Medical doctor. He was a native of Hexham and a brother of Robert Stainthorpe (*qv*), he took his degree in 1838 and commenced practice in Ridsdale Iron Works. He came to Hexham in 1841 and practiced ever since. He took his M.R.C.S. and L.S.A. in 1838. He became M.D. of St Andrews in 1861 and was elected F.R.C.S. in 1873. He seems to have been a popular person, particularly in his younger days. Also, he was exceedingly fond of hunting and shooting and of dogs. In the earlier years of his practice, he frequently rode many miles on horseback to visit his patients, often taking a shorter route across country, rather than taking the road. In 1865, his numerous friends in Hexham and Hexhamshire presented him with a gold watch and appendages and a purse of gold. In his younger days, he fought tenaciously for sanitary improvement, realising its importance from having passed through two epidemics of small pox and one of cholera. He was elected to the Local Board of Health in 1863 and served on it for eighteen years, of which, from 1873, he was Chairman for five years. By the time he was in that position, he was less forceful about sanitary improvement, taking a defensive stance over change. There was a feeling at the time that it was the ornamental to nature of the position of chairman that he enjoyed rather than the ability it gave the holder to steer the Board in a progressive manner. He was a director of the Gas Company for 41 years.

Duncan Stewart (1846-1924) (16) – Medical doctor. He was born in Blair Athol. He studied medicine at Edinburgh and soon after qualifying came to Hexham in 1869 as assistant to Daniel Jackson (*qv*). He then practiced on his own before partnering Thomas Stainthorpe (*qv*), remaining with him until his death. He then took Thomas Woodman (*qv*) into partnership. With the early death of the latter, he carried on alone for a few years, but, in the few years before his death, his nephew, Dr W. Mitchell joined him. Stewart was long connected with the Hexham Board of Guardians. For 23 years from 1897 he was medical officer and public vaccination officer for the Hexham and Slaley Districts, which included the Hexham Workhouse. It was mainly due to his persistent efforts that the War Memorial Hospital up Eastgate, which was opened in 1921, came into being. At the time of Stewart's death, it was said to be one of the best-equipped cottage hospitals in the country. One of the principal wards was named after him. He was a great gardener, especially in growing apples – his fruit won many prizes at horticultural shows.

John Sword (?-1916; 67) (25) – Station Master. He was in the employ of the North-Eastern Railway Company for 42 years, for 27 of which he was in charge of Hexham Station. Indeed he started his career as a clerk in the same station on August 19th, 1867, the opening of the Hexham and Allendale Railway. Shortly afterwards he transferred to the superintendent's office in Newcastle Central Station. He returned to Hexham in 1882. During his time as stationmaster, the volume of traffic through the station increased dramatically. When he came to Hexham, there were 14 sidings giving accommodation for 180 wagons; when he retired there were 29 sidings with a total length of 3½ miles with room for 600 wagons. During the same period, passenger numbers rose from 85,365 to 125,290, cattle from 8,575 to 19,936 and parcels from 28,605 to 71,906. The staff increased from 36 to 66. He was closely involved with the activities of the Abbey as a sidesman and for thirteen years as a churchwarden and as a member of the Restoration Committee that led to the rebuilding of the Nave.

William A. Temperley (?- 1898; 78) (3) – Businessman. He founded and ran a firm of corn and agricultural merchants that had offices and a warehouse in Beaumont Street. He and his wife, both 'natives and life-long inhabitants of Hexham', are commemorated by the Market Cross and Fountain (or

---

Fig. 11 (*across*) Part of the portrait of Robert Stainthorpe painted by Frank S. Ogilvie and presented to the Hexham Urban District Council in 1902 (reproduced by kind permission of Tynedale Council). *See page 54 for biography.*

Temperley Fountain as it now tends to called) in the Market Place, the cost of erection of which was borne by their sons and daughters.

Wylam Walker (1794-1890) (30) – Land agent and engineer, etc. For 20 years he was land agent and manager for Mr Thomas Wade of Hylton Castle. Afterwards, he was engaged as an engineer in the making of the Newcastle and Carlisle Railway, continuing with this employment until the line was finished. During this period he came to live at Orchard House in Hexham. On ceasing his connection with the Railway, he ran a large plumbing business in Hexham, together with the Corbridge Fire Brick and Sanitary Tube Works and the Dilston Tile and Brick Works. He also took over the Prudham quarries. In time, he relinquished all the above concerns except the one at Corbridge. Walker was one of the projectors of the Hexham Gas Company and was a director until his death.

Thomas William Welford (1829-1918) (29) – Solicitor. He was born in Hexham and educated at Hexham Grammar School and Houghton-le-Spring under a Dr Young. He served his articles with his elder brother Edward Davison Welford of Hexham and Newcastle, being admitted as a solicitor in 1868. He commenced practice in Newcastle but eventually removed to Hexham. His practice was extensive, especially in the courts. He was a Commissioner of Oaths. He became a member of the Local Board of Health in 1868, retiring in 1881. After the passing of the Local Government Act of 1894, Welford was elected to the new authority, eventually retiring prior to the adoption of the new ward system in 1909. During the deliberations of the Board of Health his statements were very forcibly presented but clarity was often at a premium. He was excitable and could be a most difficult member, frequently having arguments, even stand-up rows with the chairman. Once he was asked to leave because he was clearly drunk. Much of this might not have mattered but his behaviour and outlook contributed to the laissez faire attitude to sanitary problems that was to dog the Board for around twenty years. The Courant, when speaking about Welford during this period, said 'his political career has not been without a few measures of usefulness, with which it would be an injustice to deny, although he has been desperately obstructive.' He was for many years a Guardian, a member of the School Board and a churchwarden. In his early years, he was regarded as a champion of 'People's Rights', particularly with regard to fishing and footpaths. Amelia 'Countess of Derwentwater', whose claims to the Dilston estates in 1868 evoked much interest, found in Welford a staunch supporter. He acted as her legal representative when she was summoned before the Hexham Bench of Magistrates for obstructing the free movement along the Dilston Road through occupation of a wooden building.

Thomas Woodman (1872-1919; 48) (15) – Medical doctor. He was born in Haydon Bridge. He was educated at Sandyford Academy and Durham College of Medicine. He became house surgeon at Newcastle Royal Infirmary, coming to Hexham in 1898 to join Dr Stewart (*qv*) after the death of Dr Stainthorpe (*qv*). Woodman joined the Army Medical Corps and served in the Grecian Archipelago during the evacuation from the Dardanelles, in Egypt and for a year in France, where he went down twice with trench fever (caused by *Rickettsia quintana* and transmitted by body lice). In his youth he was a keen rugby player, being in the highly successful South Shields side of 1894-5. He was chairman of the Tynedale club. Woodman was a very popular person in Hexham, as exemplified by the fact that, on his death, the *Courant* devoted a leader article to him as well as the standard obituary.

Almost all the information for the above biographies has come from information, particularly obituaries, in the columns of the *Hexham Courant* and *Hexham Herald.* For some persons there have been other sources of information that are referred to in the text. The sources are:

Anon. (1913*a*) Joseph Fairless. *Archaeologia Aeliana* 3[rd.] Series **10**, 258-259.
Anon. (1913*b*) John Pattinson Gibson. *Archeologia Aeliana* 3[rd.] Series **10**, 300-303.
Anon. (1938) Hexham sixty-two years ago. II. Men of the period. *Hexham Courant* March 8.
Durie, A. J. (2002) The business of hydropathy in the north of England. *Northern History* **39**, 37-58.
Jennings, D. (2001) Restoration of the Abbey: Savage versus Lockhart. *Hexham Historian* **11**, 49-70.
Jennings, D. & Rossiter, A. (1999) Queen Elizabeth Grammar School from the foundation to the mid-19th century. *Hexham Historian* **9**, 3-27.
Jennings, R. M. (1998) Joseph Catherall of the *Hexham Courant*, 1839-1881. *Hexham Historian* **8**, 33-62.
Neilson, G. (1912) Obituary notice of J.P.Gibson F.S.A., A vice-President of the Society. *Archaeologia Aeliana* 3rd Series **8**, 37-45.
Payne, E. H. (2002) The Rev. John G. Bowran and the building of Hexham Primitive Methodist Church. *Hexham Historian* **12**, 34-42.
Ridley, E. (1863) *The Christian Living and Dying or Memoir of Mrs Hebbron by her Brother.* A. Mc Callum, 'Home Piety' Office: Newcastle

I am very grateful to Christine Hanley, Ruth Jennings, Marjorie Robson and Valerie Robson their valuable advice on the original manuscript.

Index to the monumental inscriptions in the original part of Hexham Cemetery

Ruth Jennings

I have compiled this index so that persons interested in particular surnames can locate those gravestones on which the same surname is inscribed. The two numbers refer to the list of monumental inscriptions (*see note at the end of the list*), the one before the forward slash indicating the section of the original part of the Cemetery where the gravestone is located (*see Fig. 6, page 30*). Copies of the transcription of the gravestones are held by: Hexham Local History Society, Hexham Library, Northumberland and Durham Family History Society and Northumberland Record Office. I wish to thank all those members of the History Society who helped in transcribing the inscriptions.

Browne 10/38 2/4
Bruce 4/24 4/31 4/32 4/55
Brumwell 9/15
Brydon 8/14
Bulman 5/2
Burdis 16/8 17/2
Burdon 18/10
Burdus 27/7
Burgun 1/2
Burn 11/32 2/2 6/26
Burnett 10/15
Bushby 26/15
Byne 19/11
Byron 10/29 7/30
Callan 3/5
Callender 2/18
Camidge 30/2
Campbell 27/25
Carr 30/34 30/55 30/56
Carr 30/57 8/11
Carrick 8/5
Carruthers 29/25
Carver 3/36
Casey 20/1
Catherall 3/55
Cato 11/24 11/25
Charlton 11/10 16/16 16/8
       17/12 17/2 19/2
       20/1 20/27 21/32
       23/12 25/1 25/13
       27/17 29/13 3/18
       3/24 30/54 6/16
Chester 30/53
Child 26/9
Chilton 6/15
Civil 30/41 30/42
Clark 13/18 19/28 19/29
      26/17 30/4 6/6
Clarke 27/29
Clemitson 10/33 30/48

Clerc 30/30
Coates 10/14
Cockfield 13/15
Cole 15/4
Collins 7/26
Common 15/15
Cooke 10/7 9/10
Coolden 30/59
Cooper 17/36 3/10
Corbett 20/22
Corbridge 10/5
Coulson 10/8 17/17 19/5
      2/43 4/7
Cousins 9/14
Coventry 27/23
Cowans 11/30
Cowen 13/22 15/18 15/19
      15/31 15/32 30/35
Cowing 24/9
Cowle 20/11
Cowper 28/11 28/12
Coxon 2/26 8/3
Craig 3/27
Craigie 1/18
Crawford 15/1
Crichton 5/3
Crisp 16/31
Cross 16/12
Crozier 13/14 2/23
Cunliffe 21/16
Curry 12/11 27/4 3/22
Darling 4/38
Darlington 10/25 10/28 29/5
      29/6 30/51
Davey 29/24
Davidson 18/6 3/31 4/22 4/38
Davison 16/23 21/17
Davy 21/26
De Meulenaere 10/26
Dennis 19/28

Dent 13/2 4/2
Dewhirst 27/14
Dickenson 3/38
Dickinson 27/26
Dinning 23/5
Dixon 17/26 19/3 23/13
    25/15 26/24 7/1
Dobinson 13/25
Dobson 28/7
Dodd 1/17 10/22 12/19 15/8
    16/41 19/1 2/18 20/26
    27/10 29/22 29/7 3/2
    30/70 4/18 4/45 7/4
Dodds 10/4 21/22 7/3
    8/21 9/27
Dods 9/28
Doe 23/17
Douglas 30/60
Dowley 12/7
Duncan 26/18
Dunwoody 8/2
Earnshaw 19/26
Easton 11/24 24/13
Edger 11/20
Edwards 28/1
Elliott 15/20 2/30 30/9 7/4
Ellis 22/4
Ellison 17/33
Ellott 25/14
Embleton 16/20
Emerson 30/20 30/49
Emmerson 15/14
English 1/10
Errington 18/7
Fair 10/3
Fairlam 26/13 26/23
Fairless 30/24
Fairley 6/13
Falconer 4/21
Fawcett 26/25

Featherstonehaugh 20/1 6/1
Fell 10/10 10/11 24/1 3/56
Fenwick 24/12 29/2 7/9
Field 23/16 23/3
Fisher 19/15
Fleming 11/5
Fletcher 29/24
Ford 1/16
Forrester 9/15
Forster 17/10 3/13 3/14 3/37
    3/38 3/7 4/60 4/61
Foster 30/13
Frankland 4/19
Frost 20/16
Furness 2/25
Gallagher 15/25
Gamidge 27/2
Gardner 6/32
Garland 9/22 9/24
Garnett 18/3
Gato 8/11
Gibson 21/33 25/12 27/11
    30/67 30/69 8/22
Gilbert 17/22 21/20
Gilbert? 15/11
Gillhespy 29/3
Gillies 11/36
Glenwright 2/33
Goodman 29/8
Graham 16/18 16/24 21/13 29/16
Grant 4/11
Gray 5/9
Green 1/13 10/37 2/15 20/3
    23/12
Greenwood 24/4
Greggains 26/18
Grey 7/12
Grover 16/1 17/9
Gunton 20/14 20/15
Guthrie 17/31

H ? 11/2
Haggis 11/18 12/20
Haley 16/15
Hall 7/16 13/12 13/20 19/8
    19/8 21/191 8/7
Hallam 13/13
Halliday 20/12 30/58 30/59
Hamilton 12/6 2/20 20/28 6/9
Hands 15/5
Hanning 18/1
Harding 2/1
Hare 19/16 3/41 3/42
Harkness 14/10 19/23
Harper 27/13
Harrison 13/10 13/9 16/37
    30/67 4/41
Harvey 10/38
Hastings 10/36 26/8
Hay 7/19
Head 30/14 30/15
Hebbron 5/12
Hedley 17/19 18/4 21/37 24/10
    26/16 29/11 29/12
Henderson 7/10
Herdman 10/18 10/19 12/2
    16/3 16/8 17/2
    17/7 4/54 7/2
Herron 10/16 4/56
Heslop 12/18 29/4
Hetherington 11/4 11/3 11/39
    2/14 26/10 7/13
Hewens 20/18
Hewitson 9/1
Hewitt 24/8
Higgins 27/31
Hilton 26/5
Hindmarsh 15/17 4/58
Hislop 2/27
Hodgson 21/30
Hogarth 23/10 23/11 3/6

Hogg 2/12 30/28 9/4
Holmes 27/3 9/13 9/23
Homer 30/8
Hope 1/9 12/3 12/8 28/8 5/14
Hopper 2/3 29/16 6/20
    6/21 8/2
Howard 14/9 16/32 4/46
Howe 21/14
Howey 12/13
Hudson 16/10 20/8
Hudspeth 21/35
Hudspith 30/54
Hulsen 15/33
Hunter 9/2 1/10 10/41 12/18
    3/30 3/35 30/47 9/3 9/6
Huntington 21/25 4/1
Hutchinson 2/20 20/6 26/6
    29/21 8/2
Hyslop 29/4
Inglis 7/17
Inness 9/7
Irving 16/22 21/2 27/8
Irwin 15/8
Iveson 10/11
Jackson 11/11 11/28 23/10 30/4
    30/5 30/6 30/7 7/5
James 1/25
Jameson 10/44 25/2
Jamieson 16/21
Jayes 1/27
Jefferson 30/55
Jerdan 2/41
Jessop 30/23
Jobson 30/20
Johnson 4/48 15/7 16/28 17/27
    19/24 25/17 25/18 28/6
    3/48 4/5
Johnstone 14/8
Jones 25/24
Keeling 28/8

Keen 10/21
Keith 2/9
Kell 15/13 15/4
Kellett 3/1
Kemp 3/58
Kent 13/26 25/10
Kidman 3/32
King 16/29 23/4 23/9 30/10
Kirsopp 28/3 4/14
Knight 11/20 3/36
Knott 25/23 4/44
Knox 30/45
Laidler 16/6 17/4
Lake 27/12
Lamb 21/36
Lancaster 11/21
Lane 19/21
Lee 13/3
Lees 3/16
Leighton 30/58
Liddell 15/12
Lishman 25/19 25/20 3/18 4/59
Little 4/43 9/16
Lobley 10/1
Lock 15/2
Lockhart 23/9 30/10 4/57
Long 10/34 2/13
Loraine 26/11 26/12 3/22
Lovatt 3/45
Low 4/51
Lowdon 25/18 4/53
Lowes 8/18
Luke 30/31
Lumley 15/21
Lumsden 19/21
Lyon 30/39
Macdonald 27/18
Macdougall 29/24
Mackenzie 16/27
Maling 27/22

Maltby 9/26 9/25
Marr 23/8
Marshall 12/23 16/19 2/10 3/57
Martin 16/36
Mason 6/29
Maughan 11/12 16/5 17/5 20/11
3/43 3/44
Maxwell 1/11
McAllan 22/6
McComb 22/5
McCormack 26/10
McGill 3/4
McGregor 9/21
McKane 9/8
McNaught 4/40
McVitie 4/47
Meason 2/35
Meikle 1/1
Menzies 2/36
Metcalf 24/18
Metcalfe 1/23
Mews 4/6
Middleton 24/16
Milburn 16/9 17/1 18/9 19/25
Mills 14/12
Milne 23/7 4/35
Minshall 30/23
Mitchell 12/7
Mitchison 23/15
Moffitt 30/46
Montgomery 27/32
Moor 9/19
Moore 20/24 27/28 27/30 3/33
Morgan 16/39
Morris 23/8 27/7
Morsley 20/25
Moulding 14/1 16/33
Muir 16/15 6/23 6/24
Murray 10/1 10/12 10/2
13/24 21/18

Muschamp 15/14
Nelson 4/49
Newbigin 25/17 25/18
Newton 16/41 20/35
Nichol 4/3
Nicholson 10/12 13/11 2/22
      28/5 3/17 30/36
      7/26 7/29
Nixon 3/10
Noble 6/14 6/3
Norman 10/17
Oates 13/17
Oliver 1/12 10/33 12/14 16/30
      17/35 28/10 4/29
Oliver? 18/5
Ord 21/35
Oxley 16/17 16/18
Parker 11/15 20/32 26/6 26/7
Parmley 4/4
Paterson 8/20
Patterson 10/39 15/26 16/7 17/3
      19/18 9/5 9/9
Pattinson 11/15 12/9 23/2
      23/5 26/16
Pattison 4/6 5/2
Paxton 10/24 11/27 21/23
Payton 13/3
Pearson 10/42 10/43 11/40 16/34
      20/28 23/3 24/15 25/19
      25/7 29/14 30/27
      30/69 5/10 8/6
Pennock 20/33
Percival 19/20
Perkins 3/5
Perris 29/5
Phipps 30/25
Pick 21/28
Piek 23/9
Pigg 6/27
Plews 16/11

Plummer 24/6
Polson 10/3
Porteous 10/30 10/32
Potter 21/10
Potts 11/14 11/31 11/39
      19/12 19/13 30/21
Pratt 16/16 23/18 5/13
Pruddah 26/2 26/22 30/32
Purvis 13/19 24/7
Raffel 6/30
Ramsay 4/8
Ramsey 16/39
Rant 16/20
Raper 27/9
Raven 15/6
Rawson 3/34
Reed 4/17 10/13 14/5
Reeves 19/27 19/7
Renwick 11/34 11/35 20/20
Richardson 10/24 17/14 20/34
      21/11 21/12 25/11
      4/16 7/11
Riddell 22/2
Riddle 11/16 4/34 5/6
      5/7 5/8
Ridley 11/6 19/19 2/16
      3/19 5/11 5/12
      8/14 8/15
Rind 20/29
Ritson 11/23 25/4 25/5 25/6
      25/7
Robb 13/27 13/28
Robertson 19/10 4/27
Robinson 10/23 11/22 11/27
      21/4 24/4 26/18
      4/10 4/58
Robson 8/8 1/19 10/40 11/1
      13/21 15/15 15/3 17/23
      17/30 19/19 19/6 2/21
      20/2 23/14 23/15 26/14

26/2 26/3 26/4 3/15
3/3 3/40 30/33 30/37
4/52 6/28 6/8 7/24 8/10
Rogerson 21/7
Rollingson 1/15
Rose 17/20
Routledge 17/32 20/16
Rowell 8/9 4/28 9/12
Ruddock 30/44
Russell 5/4
Rutherford 10/31 24/17 3/53
Rutter 11/16
Saint 2/29 23/19
Salkeld 27/21
Sample 6/12
Sanderson 23/13
Savage 8/1
Schmidt 3/23
Scholey 13/7
Scorer 17/29
Scott 10/23 14/2 16/38 17/34
20/11 21/38 23/11 24/12
25/22 27/1 27/27 30/1
Seaton 22/6
Shaftoe 28/2
Sharpe 20/5
Shield 11/37 3/26 3/46 3/47 4/46
Short 12/21
Shotton 29/3
Siddons 22/3
Simpson 12/1 15/16 26/28
Sinclair 2/18
Sisterson 16/14 20/19
Smillie 25/3
Smith 1/14 1/24 1/26 13/15
19/25 2/36 20/31 21/29
22/4 27/15 27/24 30/50
30/61 30/62
Snowball 11/10 11/38 21/24
23/1 9/11

Snowdon 1/20 20/8
Somerville 11/17
Sparks 19/6
Spedding 3/50
Spence 23/22 26/20
Spicer 16/14
Spours 20/21
Spraggon 23/24 23/25
Stainthorpe 12/15 12/22 20/4
23/21 30/38 32/12
Stappard 4/15
Steele 29/24
Steele 7/15
Stephenson 13/5 13/6 13/7 13/8
19/17 28/4 7/21
Stevenson 13/5 15/9 20/21
Stewart 16/4 17/6 3/11
4/30
Stobart 13/1
Stobbart 4/57
Stobbs 4/42
Stoker 23/14
Stokoe 30/9 4/19 6/5
Storey 1/28 30/25 6/7 7/14
Stout 21/25
Stowell 17/24
Strafford 5/14
Straughan 22/1
Stuttard 3/9
Summers 22/7
Surtees 2/24
Sutcliffe 2/39
Swallow 2/28
Swan 25/16
Swinburn 17/13
Swinburne 6/1
Sword 25/21
Tait 11/19
Taylor 11/11 14/6 18/7
19/22 19/26 2/19

20/33 21/8 25/8
4/20 4/37 4/49 6/18
Teasdale 16/38 3/51 4/33
Temperley 3/20 3/28 3/49
6/19 7/8
Temple 11/28
Thew 14/7 15/27
Thompson 10/32 13/17 16/2
17/8 18/2 19/20
19/4 27/16 30/19
4/10 4/13 4/7
5/5 7/21 7/25 7/28
Thornton 30/11
Todd 24/3
Tomlinson 12/10
Towns 11/9
Trotter 15/34
Trumper 15/35
Tulip 21/27
Turnbull 23/20 23/26 26/12
30/66 4/50 7/14
Turner 14/13 30/22 5/11 5/9
Tweddell 16/26
Tweddle 4/1 16/13 19/14
Tyson 26/19
Uppard 21/6
Urwin 1/5 16/25 27/22 29/18
Vipond 3/52
Waldie 8/21
Walker 30/3
Walkington 11/13
Wallace 2/16
Walton 20/4 23/23 30/12
Wancke 2/8
Ward 19/30 26/26 29/17 4/61
Wardale 13/8
Wardle 13/4 7/31 8/12
Waters 12/16
Watson 14/3 16/22 23/16
Watt 19/27 25/9

Watts 12/4
Waugh 13/16
Wear 11/26 2/17 23/6 8/16
Wearmouth 16/2 17/8
Weatherald 20/10
Weatherley 19/14
Weir 7/17
Welch 17/21 2/22
Welford 29/15
Weymes 4/23
Wheatley 10/35
White 11/33 17/28
Whiteley 16/40
Whitfield 2/25 8/19
Whittaker 6/25
Wight 21/34
Wilkie 10/6
Wilkinson 10/17 10/20 20/30
29/10 4/44 7/27
Willey 4/3
Williamson 21/5 6/10
Willoughby 24/2
Wills 24/4
Wilson 29/19 24/14 27/5 29/9
3/5 3/54 6/17
Winter 27/16 3/12
Wood 1/7 21/9 3/46 4/37
Woodman 15/29
Wray 30/69
Wright 23/20 8/4
Yellowley 27/7
Young 1/22 1/3 1/4 11/8
14/1 15/28 15/30
17/29 2/28